ENTREPRENEURSHIP AS STRATEGY

ENTREPRENEURSHIP AND THE MANAGEMENT OF GROWING ENTERPRISES

A Sage Publication Series

THE ENTREPRENEURSHIP AND THE MANAGEMENT OF GROWING ENTERPRISES series focuses on leading edge and specialized ideas important to the creation and effective management of new businesses. Each volume provides in-depth, accessible, up-to-date information to graduate and advanced undergraduates students, investors, and entrepreneurs.

SERIES EDITOR   Jerome A. Katz
Saint Louis University
Jefferson Smurfit Center for Entrepreneurial Studies

ADVISORY BOARD   D. Ray Bagby, *Baylor University*
Donald F. Kuratko, *Ball State University*
Justin Longnecker, *Baylor University*
Ian C. MacMillan, *University of Pennsylvania*
Howard H. Stevenson, *Harvard University*
Frederick C. Scherr, *West Virginia University*
Jeffry A. Timmons, *Babson College*

BOOKS IN THIS SERIES

FIELD CASEWORK:
Methods for Consulting to Small and Startup Businesses
Lisa K. Gundry and Aaron A. Buchko

NEW VENTURE STRATEGY:
Timing, Environmental Uncertainty, and Performance
Dean A. Shepherd and Mark Shanley

ATTRACTING EQUITY INVESTORS:
Positioning, Preparing, and Presenting the Business Plan
Evan J. Douglas and Dean A. Shepherd

ENTREPRENEURSHIP AS STRATEGY:
Competing on the Entrepreneurial Edge
edited by Dale Meyer and Kurt A. Heppard

ENTREPRENEURSHIP AS STRATEGY
Competing on the
Entrepreneurial Edge

Edited by
G. DALE MEYER
KURT A. HEPPARD

EMGE

Sage Publications, Inc.
International Educational and Professional Publisher
Thousand Oaks ▪ London ▪ New Delhi

For information:

Sage Publications, Inc.
2455 Teller Road
Thousand Oaks, California 91320
E-mail: order@sagepub.com

Sage Publications Ltd.
6 Bonhill Street
London EC2A 4PU
United Kingdom

Sage Publications India Pvt. Ltd.
M-32 Market
Greater Kailash I
New Delhi 110 048 India

Library of Congress Cataloging-in-Publication Data

Entrepreneurship as strategy: Competing on the entrepreneurial edge /
edited by G. Dale Meyer and Kurt A. Heppard.
    p. cm. — (Entrepreneurship and the management of growing enterprises)
Includes bibliographical references and index.
ISBN 0-7619-1579-6 (cloth: acid-free paper)
ISBN 0-7619-1580-X (pbk.: acid-free paper)
    1. Entrepreneurship. 2. Strategic planning. I. Meyer, G. Dale. II. Heppard,
Kurt A. III. Title. IV. Series.
HB615 .E632 2000
658.4`21—dc21   00-008076

00 01 02 03 10 9 8 7 6 5 4 3 2 1

Acquiring Editor:	Marquita Flemming
Editorial Assistant:	MaryAnn Vail
Production Editor:	Diana E. Axelsen
Editorial Assistant:	Cindy Bear
Indexer:	Jeanne Busemeyer

Contents

Foreword

The book you are holding is a milestone. It brings together many of the thinkers who provided an intellectual foundation for the discipline of strategic management—names like Miles and Snow, Cooper, Hitt, Eisenhardt, Amit, and Barney. But it brings them together to lay a new foundation, one for the discipline of entrepreneurship. This book can be seen symbolically as a milestone marking the second age transition of the field of entrepreneurship.

American entrepreneurship education's first stage or youth could be argued to start with the first entrepreneurship course, taught by Myles Mace at Harvard in 1947. The second stage, entrepreneurship's young adulthood, started in 1974 when an Entrepreneurship Interest Group emerged from the Business Policy Division of the Academy of Management. Pioneers such as Karl Vesper, Charles Hofer, and Arnold Cooper took the risk of venturing out to study venturing. Chapter 7 of this book, by Cooper, Markman, and Niss, harkens back to some of that early history and uses it to set the stage for the future of entrepreneurship. What ensued for the emerging discipline was the inevitable identity crisis, an effort to differentiate itself from its parent. The process was slow enough that the fledgling Entrepreneurship Division at one point was warned that its membership overlapped the Policy Division's so strongly that the smaller division might be merged back into its parent. Facing this, efforts to build a distinctive domain of entrepreneurship grew in importance. The search to find and embrace theories and researchers from a variety of disciplines became a passion of the field.

It was a worthwhile effort, and it produced a new discipline with roots and researchers from not only business policy but also organizational behavior, organizational theory, economics, technology studies, sociology, psychology, and more. The resulting voice for the discipline of entrepreneurship is distinctive because of its diversity perspective, accomplished amid a melding of concerns for person and firm, strategy and action, science and observation.

Despite this, the field of strategy remained at the core of entrepreneurship. This was perhaps most evident in the creation of the *Journal of Business Venturing*, which had as its explicit goal positioning an entrepreneurship journal high enough in quality to rival mainstream management journals. *JBV* achieved its goal largely by building on the work of strategy researchers in entrepreneurship, whereas *Entrepreneurship: Theory and Practice* gathered quality research from a behavioral basis and *Small Business Economics* did so from an economics perspective.

Pieces of this history are discussed by Cooper, Markman, and Niss in Chapter 7 of this book and by the first of the truly "brand name theorists" of strategy, Miles, Heppard, Miles, and Snow, in Chapter 6. Their contributions, building from the pioneering models of strategy, bring a fresh insight and an entrepreneurial slant that simultaneously show past and future. Their chapters close the first circle.

The third stage, entrepreneurship's middle age, is apparent in the other chapters, as the modern leaders of strategic theory provide insights designed for and based on the entrepreneurial setting. This second circle moving forward into the future is one in which entrepreneurship research can display models that openly embrace and extend strategy theory. This is possible because entrepreneurship as a field is now secure enough in its self-image and research domain that it can accept and celebrate its origins in business strategy, and secure enough in its own oeuvre of research findings that it can offer fresh and valuable insights to its parent disciplines, including strategy.

It is important to realize that today many of the questions that are most interesting to leading-edge researchers in the administrative sciences come from the situations, people, processes, or firms characterized by entrepreneurship. Whether it is decision making in high-velocity environments, as described by Eisenhardt, Brown, and Neck (Chapter 3) or the intricacies of resource modeling as described by Alvarez and Barney (Chapter 4), researchers find that the best place, and indeed sometimes the only place, in which to do breakthrough research or confront the opportunities that lead to breakthrough thinking is in the entrepreneurial world.

These findings are often so much more clearly visible when framed in the terms and settings of entrepreneurship research that what was unthinkable 30 years ago becomes imperative today. In the 1960s and 1970s, the idea that entrepreneurship or entrepreneurial businesses held lessons for all firms, including the emerging multinationals, would have been seen as the height of hubris. Today, entrepreneurship defines the new competitive landscape, as Hitt and Reed (Chapter 2) have identified, and the style of management under which entrepreneurial firms thrive can become a prescription to be taken in differing doses by all firms, as suggested by Amit, Brigham, and Markman (Chapter 5). These normative models of the environment and management are no longer controversial; they define the arena in which strategists and strategy researchers operate.

Taken together, these chapters represent the new foundation and thrust of entrepreneurship research—grounded in theory but able to contribute powerful new insights to all—researchers, practitioners, and policy makers alike. This new foundation and new thrust is at the heart of the second circle—starting here and going onto the future.

To put it simply, this book is a milestone volume, bringing together past and present and pointing the way to the future. It is a milestone for the Entrepreneurship and Management of Growing Enterprises series, but it is more than that: It is truly a milestone for the field of entrepreneurship. The ideas presented have two commonalities: They are focused on strategy, and they are grounded in entrepreneurship. It is the reverse of what was possible 30 years ago when the discipline of entrepreneurship was young. Entrepreneurship now has the intellectual depth and research achievements to make possible the beginning of a payback to its parent disciplines—in this particular book's instance, the discipline of strategy. The milestone being reached is middle age, when children can begin to meaningfully help parents. For the discipline of entrepreneurship, it was a long time coming.

Jerome A. Katz

Mary Louise Murray Endowed Professor
of Management, St. Louis University,
and Editor, Sage Series in Entrepreneurship and
the Management of Growing Enterprises

Preface

O ver the past decade, entrepreneurship has emerged as one of the most important forces in the world economy and in the study of business and management. We find that many practicing managers as well as academic researchers are convinced that organizational success (and perhaps survival) in today's hypercompetitive environment depends on flexibility, innovation, and speed. The creation of new ventures by individual entrepreneurs or existing firms is often cited as the key challenge facing the American economy today. Many large firms are striving to create strategies that are entrepreneurial, and emerging firms are recognizing the importance of a continuing emphasis on entrepreneurship in their long-term strategic vision.

Entrepreneurship has also emerged as an important area of undergraduate and graduate education here at the University of Colorado at Boulder. Colorado is recognized nationally as one of the premier entrepreneurial states in the country. The combination of a highly skilled and educated workforce, a vibrant economy, a strong technology base, and an extraordinary quality of life has enabled our state to achieve this status. It follows that it is also the ideal environment in which to pursue a rewarding entrepreneurial education. Our entrepreneurship MBA program has been ranked nationally as one of the top programs in the country. We have also developed a unique program in entrepreneurship for our PhD candidates. Our focused niche is at the intersection of strategic management and entrepreneurship. The PhD program has gained national recognition and acclaim as one of the premier doctoral programs in educating and preparing entrepreneurship professors as teachers and researchers for the future. As a result, much of our research conducted in the Management Division at the University of Colorado has investigated an area that might best be described as the intersection of strategic management and entrepreneurship.

The specific conversation about "entrepreneurship as strategy" began formally in 1994 when we hosted a conference in Winter Park, Colorado, to focus on the intersection of these two fields. Although the conference provided some preliminary ideas, the issue of entrepreneurship as strategy was still very difficult to define. To try to find a common understanding, or at least a common language, in our discussion of entrepreneurial strategies, we decided to devote a semester-long PhD seminar to the topic. The seminar was made possible by funding from the Robert H. and Beverly A. Deming Center for Entrepreneurship and our Management Division. We invited many of the top thinkers at the intersection of strategy and entrepreneurship to come to Boulder and spend several days with us discussing entrepreneurial strategies. We paired each of these renowned scholars with a doctoral candidate from our program. The doctoral candidate had the responsibility of developing a seminar focusing on the works of the visiting scholar during the week preceding the scholar's visit. While the scholars were with us in Boulder, they worked closely with our doctoral students to develop the "core" of a chapter investigating entrepreneurial strategies that built on the previous work of the scholar and innovative ideas from the doctoral candidate.

The resulting semester was incredibly rewarding for our doctoral candidates and produced the chapters in this book. We are grateful to the participating scholars for their keen insights and patient mentoring of our doctoral candidates. As we examined the written chapters and transcripts from our scholars' visits, we noticed an emerging theme of an "entrepreneurial dominant logic." This dominant logic was originally developed by Bettis and Prahalad to help understand diversification decisions. Since then, they have also related dominant logic to an organization's learning and how organizational members think about their jobs, learn to structure their activities, and interpret information from the external environment. As you will read in the following chapters, firms that are able to pursue entrepreneurial strategies are made up of individuals who constantly search for new business opportunities and enhanced profitability for the firm, in what we call an entrepreneurial dominant logic. Members of an organization create and re-create their jobs in pursuit of this greater profitability. They are constantly searching for better ways to do their job and always looking for new, profitable business opportunities in the external environment while looking for ways to improve the way they do their daily jobs.

Given the results of the seminar and the discussions that followed, we think we have made progress in linking the fields of strategy and entrepreneurship with the identification of an entrepreneurial dominant logic. We hope this concept is helpful to the fields of strategy and entrepreneurship as they search for common ground and synergistic research agendas. We also hope that this book provides the basis for an enriching and profitable conversation about entrepreneurial strategies.

1 | Entrepreneurial Strategies

The Dominant Logic of Entrepreneurship

G. Dale Meyer

Kurt A. Heppard

ENTREPRENEURIAL DOMINANT LOGIC

Many practicing managers as well as academic researchers are convinced that organizational success (and perhaps survival) in today's hypercompetitive environment depends on flexibility, innovation, and speed (D'Aveni, 1994). The creation of new ventures by individual entrepreneurs or existing firms is often cited as the key challenge facing the American economy today (Brown & Eisenhardt, 1998). Many large firms are striving to create strategies that are entrepreneurial, and emerging firms are recognizing the importance of a continuing emphasis on entrepreneurship in their long-term strategic vision.

Professionals throughout the field of strategic management have shifted their focus from static analyses to dynamic modeling. In the hypercompetitive, globally competitive world, academics and executives alike have recognized the importance of innovation, quickness, and agility for superior performance (Bettis & Hitt, 1995; D'Aveni, 1994; Hamel & Prahalad, 1994). Real-time experimentation takes the place of the relatively slow and deliberate strategic planning processes of firms (Brown & Eisenhardt, 1998). All of this presumes that the organization has a mental set permeated by an entrepreneurial spirit. Still, there is no cogent, direct

1

treatise to formally recognize and analyze entrepreneurship and entrepreneurial strategies as a new "dominant logic" in organizations.

According to Bettis and Prahalad (1995), a dominant logic can be seen as "an adaptive emergent property of complex organization" (p. 10). This book is something of an anthology whose pieces are connected by this notion of dominant logic. Bettis and Prahalad stated that

> there are many potential ties between organizations as complex adaptive systems and the concept of dominant logic, but one of the most interesting concerns the concept of unlearning. Work on systems far from equilibrium is suggestive of conditions that facilitate unlearning. Complex systems near equilibrium tend to perform in a repetitive fashion.... So it can be argued that complex systems become much more adaptive as they move far from equilibrium. (pp. 11-12)

The dominant logic of an organization filters and interprets information from the environment, attenuates complexity, and guides strategies, systems, and behavior of the organization (Bettis & Prahalad, 1995). Prahalad and Bettis (1986) originally applied the concept to explain diversification and have since expanded the concept to assess organizational learning and unlearning.

This book presents the notion of entrepreneurship as a dominant logic that leads to the creation of entrepreneurial strategies by firms. The basic premise of the entrepreneurial dominant logic is the search for supernormal profitability. This means that the firm and its members interpret, value, and act on information on the basis of the potential of value creation and profitability for the firm. An entrepreneurial dominant logic leads a firm and its members to constantly search and filter information for new product ideas and process innovations that will lead to greater profitability.

The remainder of the book builds on this premise. However, the discussion of entrepreneurship within existing firms has existed for more than a decade. William Guth and Ari Ginsberg edited a special issue of the *Strategic Management Journal* in 1990 that initiated the past decade's growing focus on corporate entrepreneurship. In many ways, this book builds on the thoughtful articles in that special issue by introducing the premise of an entrepreneurial dominant logic and adding current ideas from some of the top scholars in strategic management and entrepreneurship.

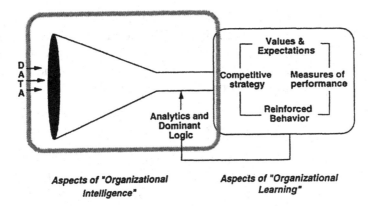

Figure 1.1. The Dominant Logic

SOURCE: From "The Dominant Logic: Retrospective and Extension," by R. A. Bettis and C. K. Prahalad, 1995, *Strategic Management Journal, 16*(8), p. 7. Reproduced by permission of John Wiley & Sons Limited.

Using a Delphi approach, this book integrates important ideas, well-known scholars, and significant articles that seem particularly applicable in the context of integrating entrepreneurship and strategic management in today's dynamic economic environment. Each scholar's individual views on entrepreneurial strategies are reviewed in this chapter. The remaining chapters of the book expand existing strategy paradigms by examining new entrepreneurial concepts that have strategic implications for new and existing organizations. These chapters are written from the joint perspectives of a well-known scholar and a doctoral candidate from the University of Colorado, Boulder.

DELPHI INTERVIEWS

Each scholar discussed the concept of entrepreneurial strategies at some length with the authors. Each had unique insights into the theme of the book and provided thoughtful insights that, we believe, support the premise of an entrepreneurial dominant logic.

Through discussions with each of the scholars, we refined the concept of an entrepreneurial dominant logic. Firms pursuing entrepreneurial strategies use human and organizational systems to screen information based on its entrepreneurial potential. Relevant information involves the identification of new market opportunities and new resource combinations that can lead the firm to above-normal rents. In each of the following sections, the distinguishing feature of entrepreneurial strategies appears to be a firmwide standard for screening information on the basis of its entrepreneurial or profit-making potential.

PROFESSOR MICHAEL A. HITT

Michael A. Hitt is the Paul M. and Rosalie Robertson Chaired Professor of Business Administration at Texas A&M University. He is the past President of the Academy of Management and recently received the Award for Outstanding Academic Contributions to Competitiveness from the American Society of Competitiveness. He has over 80 journal articles, including 24 publications in Strategic Management Journal, Academy of Management Journal, *and* Journal of Management.

There is a strong relationship between the notion of innovation and entrepreneurship, regardless of where innovation comes from. Even large firms must be entrepreneurial to be innovative. From the perspective of "the new competitive landscape," the successful firms (either large or small) will need visionary people at the top. They'll need to be flexible and a number of other things, but a clear vision is key. This vision must be entrepreneurial. Even the CEOs of large corporations must be creative and entrepreneurial. This creativity includes new organizational forms, new products, or new organizational processes. CEOs can be entrepreneurial in a number of different ways, but they will need to be entrepreneurial to succeed.

The notions of creativity, innovation, and entrepreneurship are closely related, but there are some important distinctions. It is possible to separate creativity and innovation. Creativity is having a new idea. Innovation means actually doing something with that idea, like creating a new product. Creativity can lead to innovation, but the two are not necessarily the same. It is possible to differentiate between innovation and entrepreneurship in a similar way. Entrepreneurship is more of a process. It's a way of thinking and doing things that transforms innovation into market opportunities or competitive advantage. Organizations won't be able to profitably create or innovate unless they have an entrepreneurial approach. It's difficult to separate the two ideas of innovation and entrepreneurship, but perhaps innovation is the result of entrepreneurial behavior and strategies throughout an organization.

It's difficult to provide a precise definition of *entrepreneurial strategy*, but it's possible to review several critical components. The CEO or leader must want to create something new and have a notion of what the future should look like. An entrepreneurial strategy can help attain that vision. But the key aspect of entrepreneurship is recognizing and creating a new and different future that offers greater profitability and value. Most CEOs will need to create a vision of new and different things if they are going to succeed in the new competitive landscape. Today, many CEOs at big companies are not very entrepreneurial. That's part of the problem that many firms are having these days. CEOs are too myopic. But CEOs should not get all of the blame. Corporate governance structures and reward systems often work against entrepreneurial approaches. Many compensation systems reward CEOs for short-term rather than long-term perspectives. Understandably, CEOs act to maximize short-term returns, and this really works against innovation because innovation and entrepreneurship require a long-term vision of the future.

Jack Welch is an example of an entrepreneurial CEO. He has recreated GE at least twice and maybe three times during his time as CEO. Early in his tenure, he changed GE in very major ways. He was entrepreneurial and obviously had a vision for the company that led to success. Later, there was another point when he looked at the firm and said, "We're going to have to change if we are going to succeed." He then recreated, or at least tried to recreate, that firm again. This continual recreation and innovation in the quest for competitive advantage is characteristic of an entrepreneurial CEO. There is a vision for the future of the organization, and there is the CEO who is able to recreate the firm to pursue that vision.

This may be a useful way to differentiate entrepreneurial CEOs. There are those who can't make any change at all, those who can recreate a firm once, and those who can recreate the firm a number of times to pursue an evolving vision. It is equally important to implement ideas to reach that vision. I think this ability to successfully implement a strategy to reach a vision is an important part of entrepreneurship. There is the vision to recreate the firm and then the ability to implement the changes required by that vision. There is also the ability to accept the risks that go along with changing a firm to pursue that vision. The visionary CEOs, like Jack Welch, are trying to develop firms that continuously change. Others describe firms like this as learning organizations. This is what the CEOs with entrepreneurial strategies are doing. They have a vision and are then creating changing, learning organizations to go after that vision.

PROFESSOR KATHLEEN M. EISENHARDT

Kathleen M. Eisenhardt is Professor of Strategy and Organization in the Department of Industrial Engineering and Engineering Management at Stanford University. She has recently written a best-selling book (with Shona Brown) entitled Competing on the Edge: Strategy as Structured Chaos. *Her primary research interest is in applying game and complexity theories to strategy and organization in competitive, high-velocity industries. Professor Eisenhardt has published research on strategic decision making, top management teams, strategic alliance formation, entrepreneurship, innovation, and agency theory. Her papers have appeared in* Administrative Science Quarterly, Academy of Management Journal, Organization Science, Academy of Management Review, *and* Strategic Management Journal.

The term *entrepreneurial strategy* may signal too many different things to people, and trying to label strategies as entrepreneurial can be awkward. The notion of structured chaos may be a more appropriate way to describe strategies that seek to foster constant change and innovation. Some have suggested learning theory as a way to think about innovative or entrepreneurial firms, but this is probably not quite the right paradigm. In structured chaos, innovation is strategy, change is strategy. We are trying to focus on labels that capture the organizational behaviors or outcomes that are being pursued by the firm.

CEOs seeking to employ structured-chaos theories should first focus on their current business. They should begin there and develop improvisational ideas and focus on creating a great deal of real-time communication. They should apply the improvisational model for the firm's current business, whether it's a manufacturing or service business. An interesting example in the service industry is British Airways, which is now essentially training its in-flight service people to act improvisationally. The company is teaching its people the rules, but it is also teaching them when not to follow the rules and when to act improvisationally. This is an example of a firm that focuses on its current businesses and then encourages workers to look for improvisational opportunities. Companies trying to be more "entrepreneurial" need essentially to be more improvisational around the key processes in their organization, such as product development, service development, and key training, as well as in their ongoing operations.

The second thing CEOs should do is begin focusing more on the future and create some ways or procedures for people in the company to be experimental with regard to the future. Companies typically either don't think about the future and just react or pick a particular plan or idea of how they think the world is going to unfold. Most businesses don't know how the world is going to unfold, but if all they do is react, they are always late; they are always second. Many firms need much more of an experimentation strategy that is very much an entrepreneurial strategy. Firms should go into strategic alliances where there may be new markets or where new technologies exist while looking at their product and service development portfolios. It is important that top managers add an experimental aspect to their strategy. They need to consult with futurists, and they should create a number of options for the future so the company is able to learn about the future. The company needs to have some sense of where it's going to be in the future.

The third thing I would recommend for CEOs looking for entrepreneurial strategies is to try to link the past, present, and future together. Developing coherent strategies over these time frames is very difficult for managers to do. We see new product and service development as very important. Unfortunately, we often find that this is the least understood and most poorly managed part of a company. Because this process is "undermanaged," there is a great deal of lost opportunity when businesses should be moving from one product to another. Many companies wait until cash flows from a product or service diminish significantly before they begin to make the transition to new products or services. However, in many markets today, companies don't have the luxury of making slow transitions. I like to make an analogy to the pit stop in car racing. The pit stop is critical in car racing! Top companies seem to do a good job of managing the pit stop between existing and new products or services.

In complexity theory, the technical term for this constant realignment is *patching*. Patching is continually moving the organization so business units are mapped onto the business opportunities. This is important because there is a flow of business opportunities that are constantly coming and going, converging and diverging. The role at the corporate level of the organization is to match people in the organization with the business opportunities. In the past, when things were not changing so quickly, this patching or realigning was not as important. Fast-moving, entrepreneurial organizations and their managers tend to communicate more, and they tend to communicate more about what is happening now and less about what was happening in the past or what might be happening in the future.

Firms pursuing entrepreneurial strategies experiment more than other firms. They are looking more at the futurity of projects and products. Their mix or portfolio of products and services will have more new, risky elements than typical firms. For example, an entrepreneurial strategy might have 30% of the company's product portfolio as new and unproved rather than the 10% that would be found in firms pursuing more conventional strategies. The structured-chaos idea pushes firms more toward experimentation and improvisation. On a continuum, the firm pursuing an entrepreneurial strategy will focus more on the future than on the present compared to a typical firm. The firm pursuing an entrepreneurial strategy creates more random variance by following essentially random patterns of project development than firms with more conventional strategies.

PROFESSOR RAPHAEL H. AMIT

Raphael H. Amit is the Peter Wall Distinguished Professor at the Faculty of Commerce and Business Administration, University of British Columbia (UBC). He is the founding director of the W. Maurice Young Entrepreneurship and Venture Capital Research Centre. His research and teaching interests center on entrepreneurship in independent and corporate settings and on strategic management, with published articles in such journals as the Academy of Management Journal, California Management Review, Journal of Management, Management Science, *and* Strategic Management Journal. *Professor Amit has extensive industry and consulting experience and has held a wide range of management positions in entrepreneurial settings, where he participated in the formation and growth of numerous companies.*

Many CEOs claim that the strategy of their firm is entrepreneurial. However, many of these strategies are not gaining competitive advantage for their firms. I think many of these CEOs have a certain perception of how to run the organization internally. When they say "entrepreneurial strategy," they more or less mean something that happens internally. The organization allows workers to do things, empowers people, allows people to innovate, gives people discretionary time. Compare this to Porter's view of strategy (or other strategic frameworks), where the emphasis is on the external environment, the industry, and how to compete with other firms. In discussing entrepreneurial strategies, it's always important to remember the competitive environment and the market. It's important to consider what business the firm is in and how it competes in the marketplace.

As we continue to examine the notion of entrepreneurial strategies, we'll focus more on a strategy of how we run the company internally. In many ways, entrepreneurial strategies are ways of creating nonautocratic organizations that encourage innovation and creativity. The entrepreneurial organization empowers people to make informed decisions and to take responsibility for their decisions. It forces its workers to think across functional domains, to think like entrepreneurs about the entire business. Workers are encouraged to do their jobs with the entire business in mind, so the workers must know the entire business. Entrepreneurial strategy refers to the internal organization, how we run the company, rather than to what we call market strategies.

A powerful concept to examine market strategies is the value net. A company *transacts* with its customers and suppliers. They try to buy at the lowest price possible from suppliers and sell at the highest price possible to customers. Then the firm *interacts,* as do customers and suppliers, with the so-called substitutors and the complementors. For example, a computer is complemented with software (the software product complements the hardware). Another example is film for traditional cameras. You aren't going to do anything with a camera and no film (unless we consider the introduction of the digital camera, but that is a whole new story). When you think about the positioning of the firm, you must think about the customers and suppliers as well as complementors and substitutors. This defines the competitive strategy of your firm. You both cooperate and compete with other firms in this overall context. You can have very new and seemingly strange relationships between firms.

For example, IBM and Apple cooperate in some areas and compete in others. You have firms that both compete and cooperate with Microsoft. Microsoft tried to develop its own Java language, but for now it has licensed the Sun Java language. That shows a game-theoretic view of the world, a cooperative game-theoretic view of the world. When I think about strategy, I think about strategic interaction, and I think about that long, hard, and deeply. Because without doing that, I can't think about the intent of the competition or understand the game I am playing. I think about which game to play and how to play the game. I don't just think about how to play the game. I first think about defining the game I want to play, and then I think about how I want to play the game.

When we discuss entrepreneurial strategies, we are focusing primarily on the internal organization of the firm rather than on the more complex notion of dynamic competitive strategies. Entrepreneurial strategies allow people be innovative, creative, and responsible for decisions that they make. Workers are given responsibility and trust. Competitive strategy has more of a market or external orientation, and, in my book, it has very much to do with thinking deeply about strategic interactions of the firm with other firms, firms with which it transacts (customers and suppliers) and with which it interacts (competitors, complementors). That is the view of the world and the kind of thinking that will, I think, dominate strategy in the future. In this view, competitive strategy will include planning, rigorous thought about the marketplace, and how to internally organize the firm in order to do what they want to do in the marketplace.

PROFESSOR JAY BARNEY

Jay Barney is Professor of Management and holder of the BankOne Chair for excellence in corporate strategy at the Max M. Fisher College of Business at Ohio State University. Professor Barney has published over 30 articles and is the author of Oranizational Economics *as well as* Managing Organizations: Strategy, Structure, and Behavior *and* Gaining and Sustaining Competitive Advantage. *He has served on several editorial boards, including those of the* Academy of Management Review *and the* Strategic Management Journal, *and has consulted with a wide variety of public and private organizations. Professor Barney's current research focuses on the relationship between idiosyncratic firm skills, capabilities, and sustained competitive advantage.*

We begin with the central question in the field of strategic management, "Why do some firms outperform others?" I would argue that the creation of economic rent is an entrepreneurial act because you're taking assets and capabilities that somebody (particularly factor markets) thinks are worth $10, and you are generating $15 in value. The $5 difference is the rent. The only way you can do that is to use those assets in a way that is a surprise to the marketplace. If you define entrepreneurship as the process of creating economic rents, then entrepreneurial strategy and entrepreneurship are essentially synonymous. Any rent-generating strategy is entrepreneurial. A cost leadership strategy can be entrepreneurial, or a product differentiation strategy can be entrepreneurial.

Both entrepreneurship and strategy research are focusing on answering the same question: "Why do some firms outperform other firms?" The entrepreneurship literature has taken a certain approach to answering the question "Why are some people able to start companies that outperform other companies?" Entrepreneurial strategies are strategies that earn economic rents for the firm. In developing these entrepreneurial strategies, there are some ideas that come from the strategy literature that talk about earning economic rent, and there are some ideas from the entrepreneurship literature that talk about earning economic rent. These research streams are parallel, but they are not the same. In the end, they focus on the same or a very similar research question.

The entrepreneurship literature is not clearly focused on the generation of economic rent, and the strategy literature has only become clear about that focus in the last several years. I think that much of the entrepreneurship literature has focused on the individual attributes of entrepreneurs as the source of economic rents, whereas the strategy literature has focused less on the differences of individual managers and more on differences of individual firms or industries. Interestingly enough, you can make a strong argument that the entrepreneurship literature needs more of the independent variables typically examined in the strategic management literature (e.g., firm-level resources and capabilities, characteristics of the environment). Perhaps the strategic management literature can adopt more of a focus on the individual manager such as that found in the entrepreneurship literature. I think there are many opportunities for overlap and healthy interaction between the two fields that will enrich both fields.

I visited a Japanese automobile plant a few years ago and saw some things that I think demonstrate an entrepreneurial strategy in an established firm. We toured this auto plant several years ago at a time when I was very interested in the role that strategic vision played in the entire organization. I went to the plant manager and asked him, "What is your job?" He answered, "My job is to manage this plant in order to help Nissan make and sell the finest cars in the world." This is what you would expect the plant manager to say—if he doesn't say that, something is wrong. Next, we went to a supervisor on the production line and asked him, "What is your job?" He answered, "My job is to manage this production process in order to help the company make and sell the finest cars in the world." Then we went to the purchasing office and asked the same question. The manager in purchasing answered, "My job is to manage purchasing relationships effectively in order to help Nissan make and sell the finest cars in the world."

Then I saw a janitor pushing a broom over on one side of the plant, so I thought, let's really test this notion of vision. I went over and asked the janitor what his job was. He answered, "My job is to push this broom in order to help the company make and sell the finest cars in the world." Now, that's interesting because the janitor understood his job in strategic terms, and because he thought about his job in this way, he did his job differently. Without that strategic understanding, a janitor typically finds the easiest place to push a broom and then pushes it. But when the janitor understands that he is really helping the company make and sell the finest cars in the world, he finds the places in the factory where his clean floors and facilities make the biggest difference in the quality of the company's product. Then he goes there and pushes his broom. This isn't the easiest place to push the broom, and he hasn't been directed to this area by his supervisor. He understands the company strategically and bases his activities on that understanding. I would argue that the act of recognizing your strategic role in the organization and then acting on that recognition and discovering ways to enhance the quality of the company's product or service is an entrepreneurial act by the janitor. That act is every bit as entrepreneurial in rent-generating terms as starting a computer company or software company.

Another short story might demonstrate some ways to develop these kinds of entrepreneurial people in an organization. A colleague of mine worked for a gas and oil company for a couple of years as an internal consultant. On his first day in the office, he had to make some copies. He took a look around and didn't see a secretary, so he decided to go ahead and make the copies himself. He put the document in the feeder, and just before he hit the copy button he felt a tap, tap, tap on his shoulder. He turned around, and it was the secretary. She said, "Excuse me, sir, but what are you doing?" Barry said, "I'm just making some copies—I didn't see anyone else around, and I decided I'd just go ahead and make them myself." The secretary replied, "Well, let's think about that for a second. You see, the opportunity cost for you making these copies is about $160 per hour (hourly wage plus benefits). The opportunity cost for me making these copies is about $40 per hour. So it seems to me that I should be making these copies and you should go back to your office and figure out how you can generate at least $160 per hour worth of value for the company."

This secretary is entrepreneurial in the sense that she understands that part of her role is to help this rookie at the copy machine understand that he must generate economic rents for the organization. So if entrepreneurship is rent generation, she is an entrepreneur. She didn't start the company, but she understands her job in rent-generating terms. A key question is "How do you hire or develop this kind of a worker?"

Adopting entrepreneurial strategies with a resource-based logic is having a janitor or a secretary behave in ways that are valuable, rare, and hard to imitate. If you have a whole company made up of those people, the company is going to do very well. Firms with entrepreneurial strategies must recruit smart people with values consistent with the company's values. After workers are hired, no matter what position they are in, from janitor to vice president, they should go through a training program that inculcates company culture and entrepreneurial economic reasoning and thought. The company must invest very, very heavily in the recruitment and training process. First you select them, then you train them. Then you put workers in a situation where that type of reasoning, that type of entrepreneurial spirit (the generation of rents), is rewarded, supported, and acknowledged.

Firms must provide a vision that keeps workers from going in a million different directions and doing anything they want to do. They must remain part of the firm and focused on its goals. Again, think about the resource perspective of firm resources and capabilities. For example, suppose a firm has a unique advertising capability that can be sold to outsiders. While the sale of this advertising generates rents, it also subtly or not so subtly changes the capability. When you sell the service to outsiders, it becomes less firm specific and less customized. The outsiders can now learn the capability and perhaps imitate it or improve the capability. Therefore, the act of selling these unique firm capabilities to outsiders means that firm specificity must decline over time, which means that the ability of these capabilities to generate rents internally will also decline. There are trade-offs between the ability to sell unique capabilities to outsiders and the ability to generate rents inside the firm.

PROFESSOR GRANT MILES

Grant Miles is Assistant Professor in the Department of Management at the University of North Texas, where he teaches courses in the areas of organization theory and strategic management. His research interests include the study of industry variety, alliances and networks, and organizational form. Among his publications are articles in the Strategic Management Journal, Journal of Business Ethics, *and* Academy of Management Executive.

Entrepreneurial strategies include the notion of finding the new, the innovative, and the adaptive. Entrepreneurial strategies provide an approach to being competitive. They provide a way to achieve competitive advantage at a broad level, a way to think about trying to find the new, the innovative, and the adaptive.

As firms pursue entrepreneurial strategies, they increase the demands for strategy development and strategic direction at lower levels of the organization. Firms move away from the concept that a CEO or a small top management team goes off on a retreat and returns with strategic direction for the firm. Entrepreneurial strategies become much more emergent. Strategic actions can be initiated by top management or by people throughout the firm. It's difficult for firms to find the new, the innovative, and the adaptive solely through the efforts of top management. It requires the entire organization. Eventually, a strategy will emerge from this search. If there is any strategy set by top management, it is really only a broad outline or strategic vision for the firm.

Another broad guideline set by top management might be the selection of the organizational form. The selection of organizational form is a strategic choice. This selection at its best puts a system or set of routines in place that will allow entrepreneurial strategies to emerge anywhere in the organization. A CEO can make a decision to change the entire structure or form of the firm. This change is extremely difficult to make in very large organizations. There is a great deal of deep structure, and moving the firm to an advanced organizational form is very difficult to implement. A smaller, newer firm has a better chance at changing organizational form. In this sense, entrepreneurial strategies are better suited for smaller, less established companies.

In the most advanced organizational forms (network and cellular), entrepreneurial competencies must be developed to support entrepreneurial strategies. The most important notion in developing entrepreneurial competencies is that workers must find both the market opportunity and the resources necessary to address this opportunity. Resources won't be sitting conveniently together under an existing organizational label or division. The resources may not even be in the same industry. The capability to find those resources, wherever they may be, to recognize them for the value that they have, and to pull them together is a unique skill and one that most firms don't have.

One of the first steps in developing entrepreneurial competencies and strategies is to include all of the people in the organization. Many employees want to be creative and entrepreneurial and make a difference for the company. This suggests that there is a lot more entrepreneurial talent inside organizations than many CEOs currently realize. It's important to find ways to unleash this entrepreneurial potential that is already there. Now, how do you unleash this entrepreneurial potential? Managerial philosophy is very important.

As organizational forms have evolved, we have seen shifts over time in philosophies of effective managers about workers and what they can contribute. From the writings of Frederick Taylor, we have notions of strict supervision and very precise work rules. Two more recent approaches have been based on human relations and human resources perspectives. These managerial philosophies recognize that workers are resources and have capabilities.

The human investment philosophy goes one step further in the discussion of utilizing the capabilities of employees. This philosophy seeks to unleash the people in the organization more completely. Managers look at themselves as "support," and this is something that management typically has a great deal of trouble doing. Our traditional hierarchies put managers at the top when, in fact, the pyramid should really be inverted. The workers at the bottom of the pyramid really do the work, so management's focus should be on supporting them. The human investment philosophy states that management's job is not to control and monitor and supervise. Instead, management's job is to develop the workers and provide opportunities for them to use their capabilities, including entrepreneurial competencies.

This human investment philosophy is closely related to entrepreneurial strategies. A human investment philosophy is conducive to the development of entrepreneurial competencies. It's difficult for a firm to be entrepreneurial without a human investment philosophy. Entrepreneurial activities are often the natural by-product of a human investment philosophy. It seems that managers are creating entrepreneurs with this philosophy. That's not something that typically has been done in established firms. Managers have focused on establishing guidelines and constraints on what most members of the organization could do. In the human investment model, managers are really trying to pull back those constraints and help the workers learn and develop. Entrepreneurial strategies are often a natural by-product of those types of human investment-based approaches.

PROFESSOR ARNOLD C. COOPER

Arnold C. Cooper is the Louis A. Weil, Jr., Professor of Management at the Krannert Graduate School of Management, Purdue University, and was the 1997 recipient of the International Award in Small Business Research and Entrepreneurship. His research is published in the Journal of Business Venturing, Academy of Management Journal, Strategic Management Journal, *and* Frontiers of Entrepreneurship Research, *and he has published two chapters in Don Sexton's* State of the Art in Entrepreneurship *series. Professor Cooper's current research and teaching interests center on small business management and entrepreneurship.*

A broad question that interests many organizations and has implications for academic research is "How can established organizations become more entrepreneurial?" That is, how can they become more innovative, more risk taking, more able to move fast, more like what we think of when we refer to small entrepreneurial ventures? Some scholars have called this corporate entrepreneurship or "intrepreneurship" and have typically referred to two dimensions.

One dimension has to do with arrangements where an established organization tries to grow new businesses or new ventures or at least to participate in new ventures. However, these efforts typically don't affect the rest of the organization. A firm taking this type of approach may be involved in joint ventures, may have a venture capital subsidiary, or may have a new venture management department. These may be entirely self-contained or may be integrated with the rest of the organization. These are devices that can be set up to pursue entrepreneurship by growing new businesses that do not necessarily affect the rest of the organization. The rest of the organization keeps right on doing what it has always been doing while the new venture area of the firm explores what it is able to do.

Another dimension has to do with trying to transform the entire existing organization and make it more entrepreneurial. Here a firm does not want to maintain the status quo at all. Top management has decided that it is important to make the entire organization more entrepreneurial. This can be done in several ways. Managers pay attention to making a number of things more entrepreneurial across the organization, such as the locus of decision making, performance measurement systems, reward and punishment systems, resource allocation systems, approval levels in decision making, recruitment activities, corporate culture, and symbolism.

There is another idea that has to do with the challenges for emerging, growing firms that have been clearly entrepreneurial in the past but are now trying to grow while maintaining some of the key entrepreneurial characteristics of the early firm. As an organization grows, many new people join the organization; there is a great deal more subdivision of tasks, and more established procedures and policies develop. Here I think managers should focus on questions of strategy, structure, and administrative systems that will reinforce the entrepreneurial climate they are trying to create or maintain. Here the literature on organizational stages is useful. Consider the challenges associated with the evolution of the organization and the changing roles of the CEO or top management team, and try not to lose some of the qualities that accounted for the organization's early success. I think that is an interesting area to investigate.

Another area focuses on the strategies of young firms. If one defines entrepreneurship as a concern with new venture creation or a concern with the creation of innovative ventures, then new organizations will have entrepreneurial strategies, whether intended or unintended. There will be some pattern of organizational action that constitutes a strategy. Here in our discussion of entrepreneurship, we begin to consider questions that are central in the field of strategic management. One important question is about the relationship between firm strategy and performance, taking into account firm resources and the environment.

There are other interesting questions. For example, many young, entrepreneurial, innovative firms take a lot of risks and spend a great deal of time and resources determining whether a new market exists. Once they have proven that the market is there, do the larger, more established firms come and take that market away from the entrepreneurial firm? Are there any strategies that the entrepreneurial firm can pursue that will maintain sustainable competitive advantages?

I think that strategy and entrepreneurship are very similar in the sense that they take the view of the general manager, the person responsible for the overall conduct of the business. This is different than in other subjects in business schools, where functional skills tend to be stressed. Both strategy and entrepreneurship fall under the category of general management, and they both involve developing strategies and systems, allocating resources, and balancing trade-offs across the organization.

The search for the unique competencies associated with entrepreneurial strategies is not new. Ed Roberts at MIT wrote about that more than 25 years ago. He gathered a great deal of data about high-tech entrepreneurs in Boston, including demographic characteristics. He argued that there were attributes of successful entrepreneurs and that corporations interested in being more entrepreneurial might be well served if they looked for people with that profile.

One of the things you see in the entrepreneurship literature now is more attempts to use frameworks from cognitive psychology to look at how entrepreneurs frame and solve problems. My personal guess is that this is going to be a very fruitful line of research. If large firms want to implement entrepreneurial strategies, they may need to examine the way the organization solves problems or deals with ambiguity. These are issues where data collection is very challenging.

For instance, the locus of decision making seems to be very important. Where in the organization are key decisions made? In bureaucratic organizations, there are typically many layers of management, and non-routine decisions must get approved through the layers of management. Now, there may be some good reasons for this bureaucratic system, but it certainly tends to constrain entrepreneurial activities. If the organization wants to become more entrepreneurial, I think it is important for lower-level managers to make decisions without gaining approval from various levels of management. These lower-level managers should be allowed to make certain commitments on their own.

Planning and control systems are also important. In some organizations, the greatest sin is to not have a plan. If the planning and control systems are designed primarily with control in mind, those organizations are typically not going to be very entrepreneurial. In turbulent environments, plans are often counterproductive. As an organization moves toward becoming more entrepreneurial, it will find that fewer people are planning because they are trying to do things that are different rather than things that are the same. How does an organization deal with the tension between trying to do things differently and the requirement to have some control and efficiency? There is a real tension there. Some organizations will intentionally make some core activities very bureaucratic and tightly controlled but allow some other parts of the organization to develop that have very loose controls and a great deal of slack to pursue entrepreneurial strategies.

CHAPTER DESCRIPTIONS

The remainder of this book consists of chapters written by each of the established scholars mentioned thus far. These scholars teamed with their colleagues and doctoral students at the University of Colorado at Boulder to more thoroughly review the concept of entrepreneurial strategies and associated issues.

Chapter 2, by Michael Hitt and Timothy Reed, presents a "lay of the land" overview of the causal factors affecting the current and future business environment. Key factors of technological revolution and globalization are discussed. The key features of the "new competitive landscape" include increasing risk and uncertainty, ambiguity of industry, and new managerial mind-sets. These features have, in fact, created a "new entrepreneurial landscape" requiring special entrepreneurial strategies. Specific methods for employing entrepreneurship to successfully navigate the landscape are presented, and the impact of changing factors on the entrepreneurial organization's dominant logic is discussed.

In Chapter 3, Kathleen Eisenhardt, Shona Brown, and Heidi Neck explore an approach to entrepreneurial strategy termed "competing on the edge." Competing on the edge is a shared goal of managers in both new ventures and established corporations. It represents a strategic synthesis such that managers can be effective in rapidly changing markets where they can react to change, sometimes anticipate it, and occasionally even set the pace of change. Therefore, competing on the edge is at the heart of entrepreneurial strategies.

A resource-based view of entrepreneurial strategies is provided in Chapter 4 by Sharon Alvarez and Jay Barney. One of the most accepted definitions of strategic management comes from Schendel and Hofer (1978) and states that strategic management is a process that "deals with the entrepreneurial work of the organization, with organizational renewal and growth" (p. 11). Even though this early definition included the "entrepreneurial" aspects of strategy, most mainline strategists have chosen to emphasize other areas of research, and the entrepreneurial part of that strategy definition has been diminished over time. This chapter uses resource-based theory to illustrate how entrepreneurship can be placed back in the strategy paradigm.

In Chapter 5, Raphael Amit, Keith Brigham, and Gideon Markman introduce the concept of entrepreneurial management, which, in its simplest form, is a management system under which organizational members are empowered to think and act like entrepreneurs. Drawing on concepts including resource-based theory, institutional theory, organizational processes, learning organization, and dominant logic, they explore the potential rewards of embracing such a management system. It is their contention that strategies incorporating entrepreneurial management are essential for firms striving to develop unique strategic assets and institutional capital—the foundations of sustainable competitive advantage.

The critical role of top managers in the development of entrepreneurial strategies for an organization is explored by Grant Miles, Kurt Heppard, Raymond Miles, and Charles Snow in Chapter 6. Managers must accept the development and utilization of entrepreneurial competencies throughout the organization as one of their primary objectives. It is unlikely that firms will be able to find the new, the innovative, and the adaptive solely through the efforts of top management. The involvement of the entire organization is required. This chapter discusses entrepreneurial competencies and strategies in the broader context of organizational forms. It focuses on the new and challenging role of top management in firms with an entrepreneurial dominant logic. The chapter specifically discusses the importance of strategic vision, the selection of organizational form, the adoption of a human investment philosophy for managers, and the critical roles of recruitment and training in seeking entrepreneurial strategies.

In the final chapter of the book, Arnold Cooper, Gideon Markman, and Gayle Niss explore the evolution of entrepreneurship and entrepreneurial strategies. Entrepreneurship and its academic discipline have been thriving, but will they continue to advance in the future, or will they fall out of vogue and be replaced by other hot topics? This chapter delineates the evolution of the field of entrepreneurship; it reviews its past, current position, and future prospects, noting factors both outside and inside universities that bear on the discipline. Entrepreneurship is then considered as it relates to knowledge and technology-based economy; the increased importance of services; downsizing, reengineering, and new employment forms; new organizational forms and alliances; attitudes toward small businesses and international trade opportunities; opportunity barriers; and universities as incubators. The chapter concludes with a discussion on the role of scholars of entrepreneurship with respect to teaching, funding and career opportunities, and, most importantly, research.

REFERENCES

Bettis, R. A., & Hitt, M. A. (1995). The new competitive landscape. *Strategic Management Journal, 16,* 5-14.

Bettis, R. A., & Prahalad, C. K. (1995). The dominant logic: Retrospective and extension. *Strategic Management Journal, 16,* 5-14.

Brown, S. L., & Eisenhardt, K. M. (1998). *Competing on the edge: Strategy as structured chaos.* Boston: Harvard Business School Press.

D'Aveni, R. A. (1994). *Hypercompetition.* New York: Free Press.

Guth, W. D., & Ginsberg, A. (Eds.). (1990). Corporate entrepreneurship [Special issue]. *Strategic Management Journal, 11*(1).

Hamel, G., & Prahalad, C. K. (1994). *Competing for the future.* Boston: Harvard Business School Press.

Prahalad, C. K., & Bettis, R. A. (1986). The dominant logic: A new linkage between diversity and performance. *Strategic Management Journal, 7,* 485-501.

Schendel, D., & Hofer, C. W. (1978). Introduction to the Pittsburgh conference. In D. E. Schendel & D. W. Hofer (Eds.), *Strategic management, A new view of business policy and planning.* Boston: Little, Brown.

2 | Entrepreneurship in the New Competitive Landscape

Michael A. Hitt
Timothy S. Reed

THE NEW COMPETITIVE LANDSCAPE

History has seen many events that have revolutionized the way business is conducted. In the 1970s, the invention of the microchip and semiconductor began a flurry of technological innovations that allowed the world to advance as far in communication and computing in the most recent 25 years as it had in recorded history. The course of history has produced advancements of transatlantic telephone cable, intercontinental air travel, and satellite broadcasts, all shrinking the previous transaction distance between nations and fostering increased trade between partners more and more geographically distant. It is no great surprise that computers, airplanes, the assembly line, television, radio, and transistors all make the list of historians' 10 most significant inventions of the 20th century[1] ("Ten Most Significant Inventions," 1997).

Historically, colonially and politically influenced trade practices once gave preferences to certain trade partners, in some cases even providing

---

Authors' Note: The views expressed in this chapter are those of the authors and do not reflect the official position of the U.S. Air Force, the Department of Defense, or the U.S. government.

a competitive advantage to some. But never before have these forces converged with such intensity as they have in recent years (D'Aveni, 1994; Hamel & Prahalad, 1994). Technological revolution and globalization of world business are the two key factors that have produced today's new competitive landscape (Bettis & Hitt, 1995; Hitt, Keats, & DeMarie, 1998). Further, as we shall show in this chapter, the characteristics of the new competitive landscape are now creating what is more than ever a "new entrepreneurial landscape."

TECHNOLOGY REVOLUTION

We are in the *information age*. Nua 9 (an Internet consulting and development company) estimated that by 2000, there were about 275.5 million people online worldwide (Nua, 2000). Traffic on the Internet is doubling every 100 days. Information technology (IT) industries are growing at twice the rate of the U.S. economy. Investments in IT now represent more than 45% of all business equipment investment ("21st Century Capitalism," 1994; U.S. Department of Commerce, 1998). Technology reduces the cost of resources and increases their availability. The resulting technological disequilibrium is yielding significant opportunities for those pursuing entrepreneurial strategies.

Advances in technology now allow airline passengers to shop for airline travel, select flights, choose seat assignments, order special meals, and pay for the transaction all from their own personal computer. Completing the airline ticketing process with a human representative costs the airlines money. The firm must either hire a reservations employee or pay a fee to a travel agent. After labor and fuel, distribution costs—the cost of selling tickets and getting them to customers—are the third largest expense for airlines and their largest controllable cost. In 1993, airline commissions to travel agents were $7.3 million, reaching a level double that of 1986 (Wooton, 1997). Allowing customers to do what reservation or travel agents once did reduces the reliance on person-to-person transactions, allowing for a more efficient use of human resources. The reduced reliance on travel agents has emboldened the airlines to reduce the fees they pay to travel agents, providing a competitive advantage for those firms with alternate ticketing systems in place.

In 1998, British Airways closed all 17 of its U.S. city ticket offices and emphasized to customers the convenience of booking travel on its electronic Web page (J. Lampl, personal communication, March 11, 1998). Although Internet ticket sales make up a small percentage of total sales, the trend is clear. As John Lampl of British Airways put it, "City ticket office costs are up, and customer demand for them is down. People have more access to, familiarity with, and confidence in personal computers and the Internet—the decision for us was straightforward" (J. Lampl, personal communication, March 11, 1998).

Use of an advanced technology strategy is not limited to the airline industry. Many industries are now using stand-alone information kiosks to provide information to customers. Featuring touch screens or keyboards, these interactive computer devices are providing information and making sales in department stores, automobile dealerships, banks, tourist offices, unemployment offices, movie theaters, and ski resorts. Kiosks allow customers to immerse themselves in as much information about the product as they like, while removing the pressure of a salesperson from the transaction. The market for interactive kiosks is expected to grow from just under $400 million in 1996 to nearly $3 billion in 2003 (Eaton, 1998).

The rate of technological change and the speed of technological diffusion are increasing. These two changes feed off one another. Diffusion increases technological change, and the more rapid the diffusion, the faster the technological change. Increasing change requires firms to seek out new appropriate technologies, which, in turn, increase technological diffusion (Bettis & Hitt, 1995). Research on the spread of information illustrates the increasing rate of diffusion. It takes 12 to 18 months for a firm's decisions on R&D and product lines to be known to competitors (Mansfield, 1985). Specific information is known within the industry even faster, often in less than 1 year.

The advent of personal computer access to airline ticketing illustrates the pervasive spread of information in the new competitive landscape. Customers can now examine all available flight routings, fares, and even special offers available only to those customers accessing information through the Internet. Several major airlines use a strategy of electronic notification of last-minute reduced fares to fill seats that would otherwise generate no revenue. The speed at which this information is diffused (customers are usually notified by e-mail at midweek concerning seats available for the upcoming weekend) allows transactions to occur at intervals highly compressed from those previously experienced (des Ruisseaux, 1998).

Information diffusion to customers is increasing, and competitive information is becoming more easily accessible. Research has found that the majority of patented inventions are imitated within 4 years (Mansfield, Schwartz, & Wagner, 1981) and that in consumer electronics a new product can be reverse-engineered, copied, manufactured, and shipped within 4 weeks (Badaracco, 1991).

Patents, once thought of as a firm's protection against competitors, are being used less and less frequently. In many industries (particularly electronics), it is becoming standard practice *not* to apply for patents (Rogers & Rogers, 1984). Patents rarely are effective means of protecting technology except in chemical and pharmaceutical industries (Bettis & Hitt, 1995). With the reduced use of patents, the number of patents received is no longer an appropriate measure of the success of R&D investments in the new competitive landscape.

Technology is a product of human ingenuity; it is something that we know. Thus, changes in technology represent changes in our knowledge (Mokyr, 1990). The growing use of telecommunications and computers is increasing knowledge intensity and the importance and pervasiveness of knowledge. Because knowledge is also path dependent (Barney, 1991), knowledge creation is directly dependent on the knowledge gained previously by an organization (Winter, 1987). As a result, current and future technology advances are directly dependent on the firm's previous formal and informal technological learning. To thrive in the new competitive landscape, entrepreneurial firms must create knowledge. A learning organization facilitates knowledge creation. (Organizational learning is discussed later in this chapter.) In fact, knowledge is as important as capital and labor for economic success in the new competitive landscape.

New technologies now allow manufacturers to customize in many industries, even on the assembly line, resulting in previously unavailable product variety. Freightliner Corporation has 3,000 options available from which customers can choose when ordering from the firm's heavy truck product line. Customers make selections based on their needs and choose everything from engine type to instrumentation packages. These options are data coded and transmitted to the manufacturing plant electronically, where they are incorporated into the new truck on the assembly line. Freightliner's expansion into overseas markets, notably Australia and China, is based on the technology that makes its flexible manufacturing system possible. Freightliner Chairman James Hebe secs the new capabilities as his firm's source of competitive advantage. When asked what advice he would give to his competitors, he answered wryly, "I'd tell our competitors to stay in your manual world, don't utilize technology, and we'll see where you are in 5 years" (D. K. Nicholson, personal communication, November 1997). The response to customer's demands for customization can also be seen in the previous example of the interactive kiosk. Potential car owners can now build their own virtual automobile at the kiosks, experimenting with different color schemes, wheel covers, and other options before making their final factory order (Eaton, 1998).

IT'S A GLOBAL WORLD

The second factor driving the change toward a new competitive landscape is globalization. Globalization is based on worldwide economic development and the opening of domestic markets to foreign competition through reduced trade barriers. Evidence of trade barrier removal is present in recent GATT and NAFTA trade agreements and manifest in the desire of the U.S. executive branch for "fast-track" authority to negotiate additional trade agreements. Despite recent monetary setbacks, economic development is clearly evident in newly industrialized countries such as Korea, Taiwan, Singapore, and most notably China. China's GDP has passed that of Germany and is projected to surpass Japan's in the near future (Weidenbaum, 1995). The economic emergence of these and other countries such as Argentina, Brazil, Poland, Turkey, and South Africa creates political pressure for freer markets, international alliances, and international competition.

The Chinese word for *crisis* has two characters. The first represents danger, and the second represents opportunity (Lancaster, 1997). Likewise, intense globalization presents both threats and opportunities for entrepreneurial firms in the new landscape (Hitt, Ricart, & Nixon, 1998). The threat is represented by the arrival of new competition and increased uncertainty in previously protected domestic markets. As China continues to stretch its economic muscles, the annual U.S. trade deficit with China has grown from about $15 billion in 1992 to nearly $40 billion in 1996 (Meyers, 1998). Opportunity in newly opened markets allows more growth internationally (U.S. exports to China rose 60%—to $12 billion—from 1992 to 1996) (Meyers, 1998).

The resulting market disequilibrium also presents opportunities for entrepreneurial firms (Dean, Meyer, & DeCastro, 1993). In the new competitive landscape, farmers are seizing the opportunities presented by globalization. Where those in the agriculture industry once raised crops for themselves and for the markets closest to them, they are now seeking to fill the lucrative demand of overseas markets. In Colorado, for example, entrepreneurial farmers are now raising for sale in Japan a crop that is rarely eaten in the United States. When a Japanese vegetable company representative mentioned that the Colorado climate was well suited for the production of a Japanese delicacy called kabocha—a soccer ball-sized squash—Colorado farmers seized the opportunity. Colorado kabocha is now a sought-after commodity in the $100-million annual Japanese kabocha market (Finley, 1998). Colorado kabocha farmer Bill Frye sums it up well when he says that today's successful farmer has to understand world markets: "Hauling potatoes down to Denver simply won't suffice any more" (Finley, 1998, p. 6B).

Although entry into international markets presents opportunity for entrepreneurial ventures, initial research in the area is mixed. Studies of new venture performance and the internationalization of new firms have found no significant relationship between international sales and short-term return on investment (McDougall & Oviatt, 1996). Other research has found that international diversification leads to higher firm performance and increased innovation (Hitt, Hoskisson, & Ireland, 1994; Hitt, Hoskisson, & Kim, 1997). Caloff (1993, 1994) found that firm size is not a barrier to entry into international markets and that many small firms are performing successfully transnationally.

New technology facilitates globalization, and in turn, globalization facilitates the development of new technology. New communication and computer networks now allow more effective integration of overseas subsidiaries and alliance partners at much lower cost. Technology also allows firms to more efficiently customize products for international customers at lower cost. By using new technology, small firms can now compete in international markets as efficiently as large multinational firms.

High-speed, low-cost communication systems provide links anywhere in the world, and overnight package delivery services allow supplies to arrive in real time and products to be received by international customers sometimes within a day of when an order is placed (Moss-Kanter, 1996).

FEATURES OF THE NEW
COMPETITIVE LANDSCAPE

On the basis of the explanation of the causes, we can develop a mental picture of the new competitive landscape as compared to the more traditional level playing field on which firms have competed for many years. It is helpful to view the playing field from the perspective of a football coach who must prepare for a game each week. It is a difficult, complex, and challenging job. The coach must prepare for a different opponent for each contest, with each opponent using different and perhaps unknown strategies. The coach must utilize changing resources (injured or traded personnel), and the game will be played in changing elements (e.g., the weather). To prepare for the game, the coach scouts the opponent and observes game films, looking for strengths and weaknesses of both the opponent and the coach's own team. Fortunately, the coach can prepare knowing that the field is 100 yards long, that the competition will be carried out under detailed rules administered by unbiased referees, and that the competition will start at a specified time at a definite location.

Although a manager/entrepreneur is similar to a coach, the new competitive landscape is considerably different from (more complex than) the football playing field. There are no detailed scouting reports of competitors because the company is "playing" multiple, often unknown opponents, not once a week, but simultaneously on a daily basis. Managers often find it difficult to identify competitors, much less analyze them. The field of play changes, the rules of engagement change, and the competition often occurs far from the eyes of any enforcement agency. Finally, due to the hypercompetitive nature of the environment and the combined factors noted above, managers/entrepreneurs may not even know when the "game" is in progress. In other words, they may not receive signals that the game has begun until they are "blindsided" by one or more competitors.

Whereas the majority of the "coaches" in the new entrepreneurial landscape busy themselves with firm survival and perhaps modest gains,

The New Entrepreneurial Landscape

Figure 2.1. Comparison of Traditional and New Entrepreneurial Landscapes

it is the entrepreneur operating successfully at the margins of the playing field who reaps the largest rewards. Just as the football coach finds the gains most precious inside the "red zone" extending 20 yards out from the goal line, so does the manager in the new competitive landscape find the going most difficult in the *entrepreneurial zone*. The football coach finds traversing the territory around midfield relatively easy going compared to the highly competitive, unforgiving, high-risk red zone. Although firm survival and average returns are significant challenges in any environment, the high growth payoffs found in the entrepreneurial zone are much greater.

The entrepreneurs/firms finding success in the entrepreneurial zone, known as gazelles (Case, 1996), have characteristics that help them exploit the features of the new landscape mentioned previously, while using some of the key strategies for success that we will discuss further later in this chapter. First, the gazelles are observant enough to spot a market opportunity and have the capability and organization to explore it immediately. Second, they constantly pursue increases in productivity and innovation. Finally, gazelles can quickly change organizational structure and size when required (U.S. Small Business Administration, 1998). Ironically, despite the emphasis of high tech in the new landscape, gazelles have very little to do with high tech: Only 2% of them are in high-tech industries (Case, 1996). Gazelles aren't about creating high tech, they are about *using* high tech to develop and implement innovation as quickly as possible.

Advances are most difficult in the entrepreneurial zone. Changes in the zone are most frequent and dramatic and have the most impact on the firms competing there. Given the impact of these changes and the hypercompetitive nature of the new landscape, it is clear why gazelles find the greatest success in the entrepreneurial zone.

The technological trends and impact of globalization are increasing risk and uncertainty for entrepreneurial firms. The opportunities created by the resulting disequilibrium have been noted above. But taking advantage of the opportunities presented is more challenging because it is becoming increasingly difficult to make accurate forecasts beyond the immediate horizon. The speed of change and hypercompetitiveness make forecasting difficult. In fact, forecasts of markets, industries, or technologies are largely unreliable beyond a very short time horizon (Bettis & Hitt, 1995). Because of the speed and emergence of technological change, there also are severe penalties for delay. In marginal growth industries where only one or a few firms can achieve new growth, failing to be a first mover in a market segment will result in a loss of profitable returns from that product.

The ability to take advantage of opportunities is further complicated by the emerging ambiguity of "industry." An industry is typically defined as a group of firms producing products that are close substitutes (Bettis & Hitt, 1995). Industry analysis traditionally was conducted by determining an organization's product, whereby one could determine whether a firm was in the industry or outside the industry. The ambiguity of industry in the new competitive landscape makes such analysis increasingly difficult. Take, for example, cable television service. In the past, the industry in which cable television providers operated was clear. However, now cable providers are not only in the television broadcast industry but also in cinema (pay per view), telecommunications (local and long-distance telephone service), interactive computing (Internet access), distance learning, home shopping, and perhaps more. Answering the question "What business are you in?" is becoming more difficult to answer.

The changes above require a new managerial mind-set for producing effective strategies and strategy processes. Managers' decisions often are based on their experience in dealing with similar problems. However, experience is of less value in the new competitive landscape. Managers must cope with the unexpected and *unexperienced*. The new managerial mind-set must stress constant innovation and entrepreneurial strategies. This mind-set must allow for strategic flexibility.

Organizational design in the new competitive landscape will be shaped by lower transaction costs, increased penalties for hesitancy, and competition based on knowledge accumulation. Technological advancement is driving down the cost of doing business with both customers and suppliers. The speed of change and nature of markets will not allow managers to search for 100% correct answers. Delay is likely to cost the firm the opportunity to compete. Knowledge intensity and the information age are shifting the focus of competition to knowledge and learning. As a result of these factors, the costs of monitoring, controlling, and coordinating are dropping. This allows firms to externalize functions that were previously internal to the organization and to gain process efficiencies as a result (Bettis & Hitt, 1995).

An increased emphasis on learning is also required. Information is everywhere, but organizations are struggling to use it efficiently. Instead of being able to sense change and respond effectively, managers are trapped in what Bettis and Prahalad (1995) called information-rich but interpretation-poor systems. It is incumbent on strategic leaders in this environment to take action that will facilitate navigation of the new competitive landscape.

NAVIGATING IN THE NEW
COMPETITIVE LANDSCAPE

STRATEGIC FLEXIBILITY

The pervasive characteristics of dynamism and uncertainty in the new competitive landscape require firms to develop strategic flexibility to operate effectively. Firms must continuously rethink their strategic actions, structure, culture, and investments, among other things. They must be able

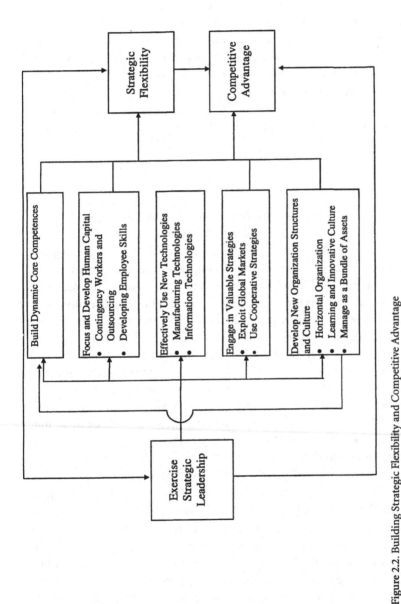

Figure 2.2. Building Strategic Flexibility and Competitive Advantage

SOURCE: Reprinted from "Navigating in the New Competitive Landscape: Building Strategic Flexibility and Competitive Advantage in the 21st Century," by M. A. Hitt, B. W. Keats, & S. M. DeMarie, 1998, *Academy of Management Executive, 12*(4), pp. 22-42. Used with permission.

to respond rapidly—sustainable competitive advantage is far more likely to come from organizational resources, capabilities, and competencies than from long-range strategic planning (Barney, 1991). Strategic flexibility is the capability of the firm to proact or respond quickly to changing competitive conditions and thereby develop and/or maintain competitive advantage (Hitt, Keats, & DeMarie, 1998). Figure 2.2 reveals the relationships among the key elements required to build strategic flexibility. As shown in the figure, firms must build dynamic core competencies, focus and develop human capital, effectively use new technologies, engage in valuable strategies, and develop new organizational structures and valuable cultures. To accomplish these tasks will require the exercise of strategic leadership. We explain each of these below.

STRATEGIC LEADERSHIP

As Figure 2.2 illustrates, strategic leadership affects all factors that contribute to building strategic flexibility. House and Aditya (1997) defined strategic leadership as the action that gives purpose, meaning, and guidance to organizations. Strategic leadership should not be confused with supervisory leadership, which provides support and corrective feedback on a day-to-day basis for work unit members. Strategic leadership affects and is affected by all other factors in the model. Strategic leaders must be entrepreneurial, visionary, transformational leaders. They must develop a vision for the organization and obtain the members' commitment to achieving the vision. The true test of strategic leadership is remaining in place long enough to see your vision realized. The reality of business is that often stakeholders are much more concerned with short-term results than with long-term vision. Successful strategic leaders will be those that combine the attainment of short-term goals with progress toward their long-term vision of the organization.

Jack Welch, CEO of General Electric, is an example of a strategic leader. When Welch became chair and CEO of GE in 1981, he immediately informed the company that big changes would be made. He stated, "A decade from now we would like General Electric to be perceived as a unique, high spirited, entrepreneurial enterprise . . . a company known around the world for its unmatched level of excellence" (Slater, 1993, p. 67). He added that GE would be "a place where people have the freedom to be creative, a place that brings out the best in everybody, an open fair place where people have a sense that what they do matters" (Hesselbein, 1996, p. 2). GE was at the time a highly profitable conglomerate, and Welch was nearly universally perceived as "fixing something that wasn't broken." He "rightsized" GE businesses, eliminating many jobs and earning the hostility of GE's workforce. He decreed that if a product line wasn't first or second in the business and didn't have a realistic chance of becoming first or second, GE would divest that business. He had leaders of GE business units answer the question "If you weren't already in the business, would you enter it today?" (Slater, 1993, p. 74). A negative reply led to divestiture of that business unit. Welch alienated many of the workers affected by the restructuring of GE, but there is no question that he recreated a firm in order to pursue a vision of a new and different future for the organization.

Strategic leadership has a key role in shaping the *dynamic* dominant logic. One way to accomplish dynamism is to build a heterogeneous top management team to develop appropriate strategies. A diverse management team provides different experiences and talents and thus allows for more effective leadership in the new competitive landscape. This requires much more than effective managerial skills. In addition to general management skills and expertise, the new environment requires knowledge of the business, the ability to develop and implement visionary change, the ability to build and maintain relationships with stakeholders, and a global perspective (Hitt, Keats, & DeMarie, 1998). Strategic leadership directly or indirectly influences all aspects of the dominant logic and as such becomes the key factor in developing strategic flexibility.

THE ENTREPRENEURIAL COMPETITIVE ADVANTAGE

Firms build competitive advantage by utilizing a unique set of resources or core competencies. Firm resources that are valuable, nonimitable, and rare and that have no alternate substitutions are core competencies that are sources of competitive advantage (Barney, 1991; Hitt, Ireland, & Hoskisson, 1999). The nature of the new competitive landscape dictates that these competencies cannot remain static; firms must develop dynamic core competencies (Lei, Hitt, & Bettis, 1996). Dynamic core competencies are developed through continuous learning, development, and redefining of organizational heuristics. They facilitate firms' flexibility and also help firms to partially enact their environment. Firms can shape their environments by using dynamic core competencies to create new opportunities. Dynamic core competencies can create new products and services that can help firms effectively compete. Thus, by building dynamic core competencies, firms can become and remain entrepreneurial. Firms that do not invest in and update their core competencies, in effect allowing them to become static, risk competencies' becoming outdated, thus limiting their strategic options in the future.

IBM is a classic example of a firm that allowed its competencies to become static. IBM's resolute position of focusing on existing mainframe computers rather than emphasizing desktop computers (a trend in the industry) eventually produced a significant deterioration of IBM's market position. The degree to which a firm ensures that its core competencies remain dynamic is directly related to the state of the dominant logic in the firm. A static set of core competencies inhibit the response capability of the dominant logic, severely narrowing the strategic options of the firm. In some cases, when a firm's core competencies become rigid, the firm must develop an entirely new set of competencies to once again become competitive (Hitt, Keats, & DeMarie, 1998).

HUMAN CAPITAL

Strategic flexibility can be developed by focusing human capital in areas most important to the firm (i.e., the core competencies). Internal human capital is focused on the core areas, whereas those positions not determined to be critical to competitive advantage may be outsourced or filled with contingency workers. Contingency workers are those who are part time, temporary, or in outsourced contract positions. Currently, about 25% of American workers are contingency employees, with estimates of future contingency worker use growing to as much as 50% (Dravo, 1994; Reynolds, 1994).

The use of contingency workers can cut costs, reduce response times to major environmental changes, and create a form of static flexibility. Static flexibility gives a firm the ability to change but not necessarily the requisite knowledge and internal capabilities to create and implement the type of change(s) needed to gain and maintain a competitive advantage.

Although the positive effects can be significant, firms must be aware of the potential negative outcomes of using contingency workers as well. Overuse of contingency workers or contracting of services yields lower employee morale, motivation, commitment, and productivity and loss of control. Just as firms in the Industrial Revolution on occasion were at the mercy of raw material vendors, firms in the new competitive landscape can lose control over outsourced functions and thus be at the mercy of their human resource providers. Firms may gain significant cost savings and create the flexibility to change but lack the internal skills and capabilities required to maintain dynamic core competencies and to create the required internal changes. Entrepreneurial firms should use contingency workers cautiously, carefully balancing the cost savings with the concurrent effects on their dynamic flexibility. It is doubtful that firms can gain a competitive advantage by eliminating workers. If they gain a cost advantage, it is likely to be imitable and thus temporary. A more competitive entrepreneurial strategy would be to ensure that existing workers serve customers better (Hammer, 1996).

Rhino Foods, a key supplier for Ben & Jerry's ice cream products (80% of Rhino's business), was innovative in solving the problem of fluctuating human resource requirements. Because of temporary changes in demand (e.g., seasonal ice cream consumption), Rhino would find itself with skilled production workers with nothing to do. Rhino found layoffs unattractive for some of the reasons listed above: bad morale, unemployment insurance expense, quality, and training expense of rehiring when demand returned. Instead, Rhino brainstormed with employees and developed a procedure for temporary exchanges of employees with other companies with fluctuating human resource requirements (U.S. Small Business Administration, 1998).

Technological and other requisite knowledge necessary for operating the firm is stored within the firm's human resources. Purchased inputs are combined with human resource capabilities to create new technology and other outputs. Thus, human knowledge and skills are required to make the types of changes needed to gain competitive advantage. To ensure that firms' human resource capabilities are dynamic, a continuing investment in human capital is required. Research reveals that the United States may be lagging far behind in such investment, spending as little as one fifth the amount invested by European firms in employee training and development

(Useem, 1996). Continuous development of human capital helps create dynamic strategic flexibility, whereas outsourcing and use of contingency workers creates only static flexibility.

Human capital is critical for taking advantage of the emerging technology. To implement and effectively use new technologies requires human knowledge and skills. Thus, continuous development of human capital may be required to participate in the technological revolution (U.S. Department of Commerce, 1998).

EMERGING TECHNOLOGY

Effective use of emerging technology can also help to create and maintain strategic flexibility. New manufacturing technologies, similar to those used by Freightliner, have increased the ability of firms to customize products and provide more product variety. Technology advances now enable firms to combine strategies of low cost and high quality for different markets.

Furthermore, the use of up-to-date sophisticated information and communication technology is critical for maintaining strategic flexibility. The examples of on-line airline reservations systems and interactive kiosks cited earlier illustrate the use of information technology to create competitive advantage. New technology can contribute to strategic flexibility, increase access to products, reduce costs of coordination across internal units and geographic boundaries, and increase the speed of actions taken.

ENTREPRENEURIAL COOPERATION
AND GLOBALIZATION

Exploiting global markets and using cooperative strategies are two actions that contribute to strategic flexibility through entrepreneurial strategy creation and implementation. The increased presence of foreign firms in domestic markets creates substantial pressure for domestic firms to compete in international markets. The trend toward global markets is illustrated by small businesses participation in international competition. Since 1990, the number of small businesses in the United

States competing in global markets has increased substantially, from 20% to 50% (Hitt & Bartkus, 1997).

Certainly, entrepreneurial firms with significant growth have begun to seek international markets. For example, Starbucks, with its phenomenal growth in recent years, is now moving into Asian markets. Starbucks' move also has implications for its suppliers such as Expresso Armando, founded in 1993. Armando is the premier manufacturer of espresso machines. Starbucks' move into international markets is likely to produce sales of 200 espresso machines for Starbucks' overseas operations (Expresso Armando, 1998).

The concept of a multinational firm operating as a collection of independent subunits should give way to that of a transnational firm integrating activities across national borders (Bartlett & Ghoshal, 1989). Transnational firms can provide global coordination and collaboration while maintaining local independence to maximize international opportunities for growth. Effective use of emerging information and communication technology allows effective transnational operation while reducing the cost of international competition (Bartlett & Ghoshal, 1989).

Strategic alliances are becoming one of the most popular methods of entry into international markets (Dacin, Hitt, & Levitas, 1997). Partners in strategic alliances share costs and contribute core competencies to the cooperative arrangement. The benefits of the alliance include greater use of technology, more access to capital, localized knowledge of international markets, and greater managerial experience.

There are also disadvantages to alliances. Partners may become significant competitors after the arrangement is terminated. There are also substantial monitoring costs in alliances that can offset the gains available. In addition or as an alternative to alliances, firms may choose to use R&D consortia, which combine resources and knowledge to develop and transfer technology, or interorganizational networks, which allow entrepreneurial firms to negate some of the resource and market power of large firms.

Cooperative strategies are important for entrepreneurial firms in particular. Entrepreneurial firms must exploit their social capital to succeed in international markets. Entrepreneurial firms use formal and informal networks for mutual support and to combine resources and knowledge to enter and successfully operate in international markets. In fact, research has shown that entrepreneurial firms participating in a broader range of organizational networks experience more growth than those with less participation in such networks (Zhao & Aram, 1995). Entrepreneurial networks include informal relationships (e.g., personal relationships) and formal relationships (e.g., long-term cooperative arrangements such as joint ventures or subcontracting arrangements). Often, informal relationships precede formal relationships, particularly in international markets. Informal relationships allow partners to develop knowledge, understanding, and trust of their partners (Hara & Kanai, 1994). Informal networks supply important information to entrepreneurial firms and frequently evolve over time into more formal arrangements. Whether formal or informal, these networks often are critical for entrepreneurial firms because they need partner organizations for market knowledge and access, as well for the resources to enter and sustain operations in those markets (Hitt & Bartkus, 1997).

Extending networks into international markets requires increased knowledge of other cultures. For example, although Chinese and Korean entrepreneurs exhibit several characteristics similar to those of U.S. entrepreneurs, such as achievement, independence, and self-determination, they also exhibit some differences, such as investing more of their own equity, borrowing more from family and friends and less from financial institutions, and making higher profits (Bates, 1997). The differences are important because Chinese and Korean entrepreneurs may expect more equity to be invested in a joint venture than U.S. entrepreneurs may desire, for example.

Final ways in which entrepreneurial leaders can build dynamic flexibility and successfully navigate the competitive landscape are by developing new organizational structures and cultures. Horizontal firm structures and innovative and learning cultures facilitate coordination and collaboration.

When considering organizational structure, firms should heed a cross-cultural caveat. Although flattening organizations and empowering workers may seem like an intuitively obvious step to the Western (specifically U.S.) reader, the strategy may not prove as successful elsewhere. In cultures with more power distance, for example, where workers expect direction from a superior, the extra management layer may be required to avoid cultural conflict. This is not to say that a move toward a more horizontal organization will not prove beneficial, but the optimum number of layers in the organization may differ by culture.

ENTREPRENEURIAL STRUCTURES

Traditional vertical structures with sequential operations and coordination requirements lengthen reaction time and often hinder technological development. The requirement for speed and technology development in the new competitive landscape calls for alternative structures. A flattened, horizontal organization is often more time efficient and more productive (Hitt, Nixon, Hoskisson, & Kochhar, 1998). Firms that implement such structures, however, face the challenge of creating new mind-sets for workers familiar with the traditional vertical hierarchy. Independent frames of reference must be removed and replaced with a cross-functional, entrepreneurial view of the firm. Creating groups with different perspectives is one way to effect this change. Mixed-experience autonomous work teams are often more creative and develop new products faster than more traditional groups (Hitt, Hoskisson, & Nixon, 1993; Woodman, Sawyer, & Griffin, 1993). Workers must also learn to think entrepreneurially—as if they were the owners of the company. As Hammer (1996) wrote:

> Our new role model is no longer the corporate manager but the entrepreneur. No one needs to tell the small company owner of the need to stay close to the customer, to remain flexible, to reduce non-value-adding overhead, to respond quickly to new situations . . . that success at one thing means nothing without success at everything else. (p. 31)

Advances in technology have served to customize groups even further. Through communication and information network systems, firms can now create virtual teams with members who reside in dispersed physical locations. Thus, the horizontal structure can help firms develop strategic flexibility by fostering increased innovation and shortening decision-making time lines.

ENTREPRENEURIAL CULTURE

Creating a culture within the firm in which organizational learning is a fundamental base is critical for maintaining competitiveness in the new competitive landscape. Organizations driven by the need for continuous innovation, the speed of technological diffusion, and the need to respond quickly to a changing environment must have organizational learning as a dynamic core competence to remain competitive. Recall that innovation is the creation of new knowledge. Entrepreneurial firms use learning organizations to create knowledge by converting learning into firm-specific resources and skills (Hitt & Bartkus, 1997). Creativity should not be confused with innovation—having a new idea is not enough unless it is further developed into a new product, service, process, or activity. Only by following through on the creative process can entrepreneurial organizations foster higher levels of innovation. An important source of sustained competitive advantage is knowledge. Knowledge allows the firm to meet changing market demands with new technologies. Only by continuous adaptation through learning can firms avoid the penalties of delay. For in the new competitive landscape, the firm that falls behind competition may well find it impossible to recapture a competitive advantage.

Although the fast-paced nature of the new competitive landscape is critical to entrepreneurial firms, it is interesting to note that the environment has evolved to the point where it may not be possible for entrepreneurs to gain a competitive advantage with a time-based strategy. Making and implementing strategic decisions quickly (Eisenhardt, 1990) and increasing speed to marketplace (Sheridan, 1994) are thought to be important competitive assets. But research on high-growth entrepreneurial firms has shown that time-based strategies are irrelevant for these types of firms due to the characteristics within the group (Ireland & Hitt, 1997). Though time-based strategies may allow entrepreneurs to compete effectively with larger, less flexible firms, they do not seem to provide an advantage within the group of entrepreneurial firms. Rather, a time-based strategy may be a prerequisite to join and remain in the competitive ball game. A focus on low-cost or high-quality strategies may have a stronger positive effect on firm performance.

ENTREPRENEURIAL BUNDLES

One entrepreneurial strategy that shows promise for entrepreneurial firms is managing firms as a bundle of assets. Firms must be prepared to enter and exit businesses quickly as markets emerge and fade. Rather than employing the traditional practice of managing a portfolio of assets in which the stability of factors such as risk is assumed, firms can manage a bundle of assets. These bundles can be aggregated, disaggregated, or reconfigured quickly to respond to changes in the environment (Hitt, Keats, & DeMarie, 1998). Firms must move away from an asset portfolio structure with a short-term focus toward that of loosely coupled bundles of assets (Orton & Weick, 1990). This can be accomplished by using a subsidiary structure that allows for significant autonomy within each subsidiary. Subsidiaries are linked through common corporate culture and reporting systems, thereby forming a network organization. The autonomy combined with network linkages allows for the development of learning within each subsidiary and for long-term investment in local dynamic core competencies and innovative culture valuable in specific market conditions. It also allows the subsidiary to develop as an independent organization capable of standing alone should divestiture become necessary.

THE DOMINANT LOGIC IN THE NEW COMPETITIVE LANDSCAPE

The dominant logic of a firm (or entrepreneur) will be affected significantly by the new competitive landscape. As previously discussed in this book, Prahalad and Bettis (1986) defined the dominant logic as the way in which managers conceptualize the business and make critical resource allocation decisions. Of particular importance in the hypercompetitive environment of the new competitive landscape is the role of unlearning. The dominant logic represents the optimum for the firm in its immediate environment. Rarely can it represent, however, a long-term or global optimum. In other words, firms often build an internal environment based on past and current experience, not necessarily anticipating the future. For this reason, the dominant logic is suited to the present but needs to be changed to effectively manage new challenges when they arise. When environmental factors change, a new dominant logic may need to be developed quickly.

Developing a new dominant logic necessitates first unlearning the existing dominant logic (Bettis & Prahahlad, 1995). Crucial to unlearning is the length of time the current dominant logic has been in place. In the new competitive landscape, a firm allowing its dominant logic to remain stable over long periods may find it more difficult to unlearn and create a new dominant logic to keep pace with the fast-changing environment.

In their extension of dominant logic, Bettis and Prahalad (1995) described the change process as rolling a ball out of a valley with hills on each side. Changing the mind-set becomes harder over time as the valley becomes deeper and the hills become mountains. The longer a dominant logic is in place, the harder changing it becomes. One strategy for overcoming the obstacles to change is to make change a regular part of the organization's strategy. Nearly 20 years ago, Peter Drucker (1980) recommended that firms incorporate "planned abandonment." A fresh look at Drucker's (1980) call for "a systematic abandonment policy at all times, sloughing off the past so that resources are available for the future" (p. 55), seems more appropriate than ever given the new landscape of the future.

Through planned abandonment, an organization makes recurring examination and recreation a part of the firm's culture and reduces the barriers to changing quickly when the landscape demands it. Thus, to develop dynamic core competencies, a firm must first develop a *dynamic dominant logic*. In this way, a dynamic dominant logic can serve as a competitive advantage to help meet the challenges presented by the new competitive landscape.

FLEXIBILITY OF THE ORGANIZATION

Smaller and newer entrepreneurial firms are probably the most flexible. They are also quite important to the U.S. economy. It has been estimated that about 3.5 million new businesses are created in the United States each year. These new firms take significant risk but also take advantage of significant opportunities. Entrepreneurship is similar to the Chinese word for *crisis* as discussed earlier. Because of their flexibility, entrepreneurial firms take risks to take advantage of opportunities. Thus, these firms are frequently on the cutting edge of their industries. One example is Wawa Inc. Wawa started as a family dairy and has grown into an interstate chain of new-concept convenience stores. Wawa's stores carry such products as kiwi, cappucino, and pasta salad. They also serve Taco Bell burritos and Pizza Hut pizza. Wawa founded its first store in 1985 and now enjoys sales of approximately $850 million (Westfeldt, 1997).

The Roman Empire used the largest river in Europe, the Rhine, as a protective northern dividing line between the empire and the barbarian tribes on the other side. In 406 A.D., the Rhine froze solid, allowing the barbarians on the far side to cross the river and attack the Roman army on the other side (Cahill, 1995). As a result, the Romans, having conducted business as usual for 11 centuries, found their empire under assault and would soon see it fall. Those firms with static strategies based on the past should heed this warning: The water temperature in the protective moat separating the traditional level playing field from the new competitive landscape is rapidly dropping. Entrepreneurial firms exist on the other side of the moat awaiting the freeze. If the moat does not freeze, they are building craft to cross the moat and challenge for leadership in the next millennium.

NOTE

1. Results of a survey of 100 U.S. history professors on the century's most significant people inventions and events, conducted by Siena College Research Institute in Loudenville, N.Y.

REFERENCES

Badaracco, J. L., Jr. (1991). *The knowledge link: How firms compete through strategic alliances.* Boston: Harvard Business School Press.

Barney, J. (1991). Firm resources and the theory of competitive advantage. *Journal of Management, 17,* 99-120.

Bartlett, C. A., & Ghoshal, S. (1989). *Managing across borders: The transnational solution.* Boston: Harvard Business School Press.

Bates, T. (1997). Financing small business creation: The case of Chinese and Korean immigrant entrepreneurs. *Journal of Business Venturing, 12,* 109-124.

Bettis, R. A., & Hitt, M. A. (1995). The new competitive landscape. *Strategic Management Journal, 16,* 7-19.

Bettis, R. A., & Prahalad, C. K. (1995). The dominant logic: Retrospective and extension. *Strategic Management Journal, 16*(1), 5-14.

Cahill, T. (1995). *How the Irish saved civilization.* New York: Doubleday.

Caloff, J. L. (1993). The impact of size on internationalization. *Journal of Small Business Management, 31*(4), 60-69.

Caloff, J. L. (1994). The relationship between firm size and export behavior revisited. *Journal of International Business Studies, 25,* 367-387.

Case, J. (1996). The age of the gazelle. *Inc., 18*(7), 44-45.

Dacin, M. T., Hitt, M. A., & Levitas, E. (1997). Selecting partners for successful international alliances: Examination of U.S. and Korean firms. *Journal of World Business, 32*, 3-16.

D'Aveni, R. A. (1994). *Hypercompetition.* New York: Free Press.

Dean, T., Meyer, G. D., & DeCastro, J. (1993, Winter). Determinants of new-firm formations in manufacturing industries: Industry dynamics, entry barriers, and organizational inertia. *Entrepreneurship Theory and Practice,* pp. 49-60.

des Ruisseaux, R. (1998, February 16). Have computer, you can travel. *Denver Post,,* p. 3C.

Dravo, E. (1994). How to play the jobs recovery. *Financial World, 163*(7), 121.

Drucker, P. F. (1980). Managing for tomorrow: Managing in turbulent times. *Industry Week, 20*(1), 54-64.

Eaton, J. (1998, February 15). Soft sell: Kiosks ease car shopping. *Denver Post,* p. 11.

Eisenhardt, K. M. (1990). Speed and strategic choice: How managers accelerate decision making. *California Management Review, 32*(3), 39-54.

Expresso Armando. (1998, January 19). *The EM launch pad.* www.benlore.com.

Finley, B. (1998, February 5). Where does your garden go: Farmers thinking globally. *Denver Post,* p. 6B.

Hamel, G., & Prahalad, C. K. (1994). *Competing for the future.* Boston: Harvard Business School Press.

Hammer, M. (1996). The new loyalty. *Leader to Leader, 2,* 30-35.

Hara, G., & Kanai, T. (1994). Entrepreneurial networks across oceans to promote international strategic alliances for small businesses. *Journal of Business Venturing, 9,* 489-507.

Hesselbein, F. (1996). Managing in a world that is round. *Leader to Leader, 2,* 6-8.

Hitt, M. A., & Bartkus, B. A. (1997). International entrepreneurship. In J. A. Katz & R. H. Brockhaus, Sr. (Eds.), *Advances in entrepreneurship, firm emergence and growth.* Greenwich, CT: JAI.

Hitt, M. A., Hoskisson, R. E., & Ireland, R. A. (1994). A mid-range theory of the interactive effects of international and product diversification on innovation and performance. *Journal of Management, 20,* 297-326.

Hitt, M. A., Hoskisson, R. E., & Kim, H. (1997). International diversification: Effects on innovation and firm performance in product diversified firms. *Academy of Management Journal, 40,* 767-798.

Hitt, M. A., Hoskisson, R. E., & Nixon, R. D. (1993). A mid-range theory of interfunctional integration, its antecedents and outcomes. *Journal of Engineering and Technology Management, 10,* 161-185.

Hitt, M. A., Ireland, R. D., & Hoskisson, R. E. (1999). *Strategic management: Competitiveness and globalization.* Cincinnati, OH: Southwestern.

Hitt, M. A., Keats, B. W., & DeMarie, S. M. (1998). Navigating in the new competitive landscape: Building strategic flexibility and competitive advantage in the 21st century. *Academy of Management Executive, 12*(4), 22-42.

Hitt, M. A., Nixon, R. D., Hoskisson, R. E., & Kochhar, R. (1999). Corporate entrepreneurship and cross-functional fertilization: Activation, process and disintegration of a new product design team. *Entrepreneurship: Theory and Practice, 23*(3), 145-167.

Hitt, M. A., Ricart, J. E., & Nixon, R. D. (1998). The new frontier. In M. A. Hitt, J. E. Ricart, & R. D. Nixon (Eds.), *Managing strategically in an interconnected world.* New York: John Wiley.

House, R. J., & Aditya, R. N. (1997). The social scientific study of leadership: Quo vadis? *Journal of Management, 23,* 409-473.

Ireland, R. A., & Hitt, M. A. (1997). Performance strategies for high-growth entrepreneurial firms. In P. D. Reynolds, W. D. Bygrave, N. M. Carter, P. Davidsson, W. B. Gartner, C. M.

Mason, & P. P. McDougall (Eds.), *Frontiers of entrepreneurship research*. Wellesley, MA: Babson College.

Lancaster, H. (1997, August 29). A company crisis could be a chance to make your mark. *Wall Street Journal*. Http//www.wsj.com/edition/current/articles.

Lei, D., Hitt, M. A., & Bettis, R. A. (1996). Dynamic core competences through meta-learning and strategic context. *Journal of Management, 22*, 549-569.

Mansfield, E. (1985, December). How rapidly does new technology leak out? *Journal of Industrial Economics, 33*, 217-223.

Mansfield, E., Schwartz, M., & Wagner, S. (1981, December). Imitation costs and patents: An empirical study. *Economic Journal, 91*, 907-918.

McDougall, P. P., & Oviatt, B. M. (1996). New venture internationalization, strategic change, and performance: A follow-up study. *Journal of Business Venturing, 11*(1), 23-40.

Meyers, D. (1998, February 8). Open for business: World's largest market offers huge risks, rewards. *Denver Post*, p. 1J.

Mokyr, J. (1990). *The lever of riches: Technological creativity and technological progress*. New York: Oxford University Press.

Moss-Kanter, R. (1996). How locals can win global contests. *Leader to Leader, 1*, 25-29.

Nua (2000). Retrieved from the World Wide Web, February 18, 2000, at http://www.nua.ie/ surveys/how_many_online/index.html.

Orton, J. D., & Weick, K. E. (1990). Loosely coupled systems: A reconsideration. *Academy of Management Review, 15*, 203-223.

Prahalad, C. K., & Bettis, R. A. (1986). The dominant logic: A new linkage between diversity and performance. *Strategic Management Journal, 7*, 485-501.

Reynolds, L. (1994). Washington confronts part-time America. *Management Review, 83*(2), 27-28.

Rogers, E. M., & Rogers, J. K. (1984). *Silicon Valley fever*. New York: Basic Books.

Sheridan, J. H. (1994, December 19). A CEO's perspective on innovation. *Industry Week*, pp. 11-14.

Slater, R. I. (1993). *The new G.E.: How Jack Welch revived an American institution*. Homewood, IL: Business One Irwin.

The ten most significant inventions of the 20th century. (1997, November 19). *Denver Post*, p. 12A.

21st century capitalism: Snapshot of the next century [Special issue]. (1994, June). *Business Week*.

U.S. Department of Commerce. (1998). *The emerging digital economy*. Washington, DC: Secretariat of Electronic Commerce.

U.S. Small Business Administration. (1998). *High growth companies: Doing it faster, better and cheaper*. Washington, DC: Secretariat of Electronic Commerce.

Useem, M. (1996). Corporate education and training. In C. Kaysen (Ed.), *The American corporation today*. New York: Oxford University Press.

Weidenbaum, M. (1995). The changing U.S. role in Asia. *Executive Speeches, 9*(4), 17-19.

Westfeldt, A. (1997, December 25). Convenience stores in the 90s: Wawa redefines an American institution. *Waco Herald Tribune*, p. C5.

Winter, S. G. (1987). Knowledge and competence as strategic assets. In D. J. Teece (Ed.), *The competitive challenge*. Cambridge, MA: Ballinger.

Woodman, R. W., Sawyer, J. E., & Griffin, R. W. (1993). Toward a theory of organizational creativity. *Academy of Management Review, 18*, 293-321.

Wooton, S. (1997, October 26). Travelers, agencies are feeling impact of commission cut. *Denver Post*, p. 6T.

Zhao, L., & Aram. J. D. (1995). Networking and growth of young technology-intensive ventures in China. *Journal of Business Venturing, 10*, 349-370.

3 | Competing on the Entrepreneurial Edge

Kathleen M. Eisenhardt
Shona L. Brown
Heidi M. Neck

"Wear sunscreen." This is how Kurt Vonnegut is supposed to have opened his mythical commencement address to the MIT graduating class of 1997. He purportedly continued, "If I could offer you only one tip for the future, sunscreen would be it. The long term benefits of sunscreen have been proved by scientists. . . ." But although the fantasy speech by Vonnegut is now firmly entrenched in urban myth, there is perhaps no other advice on the future that could be dispensed with such certainty. Yet maybe the fact that there is so much uncertainty is a good thing. Uncertainty breeds change, and change, when strategically managed, can drive innovation, entrepreneurship, and growth.

Organizations of all sizes and in many industries are now competing in what Bettis and Hitt (1995) termed the new competitive landscape. This business environment is characterized by increasing risk, decreasing ability to forecast, fluid firm and industry boundaries, a managerial mind-set that demands unlearning many traditional management practices, and fresh organizational and even "disorganizational" forms that allow managers to sense, respond to, and even create change. Yet although the new competitive landscape has created a plethora of opportunities, current management perspectives and tools offer little direction for seizing them.

Coping with immense change is the dominant feature of managing in the new competitive landscape. Consider the following from *The Paradox Principles* (Price Waterhouse, 1996):

> The pressures on today's managers and employees are unprecedented. For many of us, the sum of our institutional learning took place in an environment much different than we will face in the decade ahead. The playing field was level, if not pitched to our advantage. Many of the rules were obvious. Structure was our friend. Hierarchy provided context and orientation. Time helped, and there was enough. Uncertainty was to be avoided. It's not that the rules have been tinkered with. We're in a different game! We've honed our cricket skills and suddenly find we're in a basketball game, where little more than gravity can be counted on. It's not simply that the pace has increased. Our "velocity"—measured in air miles, e-mail messages, and meetings—is approaching some point beyond which human beings should not go. (p. 4)

Complexity is another critical aspect in today's business environment because change is coming from so many different directions. There are new computer technologies, markets, financial systems, demographic patterns, emotional requirements for managing, and communication networks. Competitors come and go. Customer groupings are shifting and becoming more differentiated. Complementary products and services are critical to the success of many firms. Competition importantly involves not only the traditional head-to-head competition with competitors but also collaboration with partnering firms. The net effect is that there is simply much more to manage than in the past.

Chaos is part of the picture as well. The common-language meaning of the term *chaos* is "confusion," and confusion does describe the new business landscape. But the scientific use of the term is perhaps even more descriptive. Chaos theory describes systems with outcomes that are governed by nonlinear differential equations. The principal managerial implication of chaos theory is that small changes or shocks to the system can have major impact. Therefore, there is a so-called "sensitive dependence on initial conditions," meaning that causality is difficult to understand and that the scale effects of change are largely unpredictable. A classic illustration of these effects is the butterfly effect noted by Lorenz. A butterfly flapping its wings, a seemingly minor event in the United States, can influence weather patterns in Japan (Bygrave, 1989). Stacey (1996) described the phenomenon in a less colorful but perhaps more accurate fashion: "Under conditions of nonlinearity and randomness, incremental changes that may themselves seem insignificant can precipitate major discontinuous or qualitative change because of the emergent properties triggered by marginal adjustments" (p. 265).

Finally, managing paradox is critical to managing in the new competitive landscape. As Collins and Porras (1994) wrote, "The tyranny of the OR pushes people to believe that things must be either A OR B, but not both" (p. 43). They then argued that such exclusionary thinking is wrongheaded. Rather, managers should embrace contradiction by replacing "OR" with "AND."

ENTREPRENEURIAL OPPORTUNITIES

Although the new competitive landscape offers many managerial challenges, it also offers enormous opportunities. Economists from the Austrian school are particularly eloquent in their description of these (see Jacobson, 1992, for a review). They argue that entrepreneurial discovery in states of disequilibrium can lead to above-average returns in the marketplace. The argument is one of recurring "waves of creative destruction." That is, entrepreneurs begin the process by engaging in actions that capitalize on the opportunities that result from innovations. These actions then destabilize markets and destroy the advantages of established firms. Eventually, however, these actions are imitated by managers in other firms, and finally markets return to equilibrium until the next wave of innovations begins the process again (Jacobson, 1992; Schumpeter, 1934). This view suggests that the innovation and change that are characteristic of today's markets drive successive waves of entrepreneurial opportunities. So for today's managers, survival may be the first step, but reinvention, growth, and even market dominance are the real goals.

Moreover, we think that these opportunities for capitalizing on change are not confined to the classically defined "entrepreneurial" firm. Entrepreneurial strategy goes beyond the founders and managers of new ventures. Increasingly, managers within established firms are seeing themselves as entrepreneurs—not just by choice but also by necessity. Entrepreneurial strategy is no longer just for new ventures.

Yet although both sets of managers may, in fact, be entrepreneurs, their paths to successful entrepreneurial strategy usually differ. For the manager of a new venture, the starting point is typically a chaotic organization with minimal structure and a time orientation that hypnotically centers on the future. For the manager of an established firm, the starting point is typically a bureaucratic organization with a rigid structure and a tendency to stay locked in the past.

PLAN OF THE CHAPTER

This chapter has two purposes. The first is to describe the "competing on the edge" approach to entrepreneurial strategy (Brown & Eisenhardt, 1998). This approach is based on a combination of extensive field research and leading-edge science surrounding the fundamental nature of change. Our underlying argument is that competing on the edge is the shared destination of managers in both new ventures and established corporations. It represents the strategic synthesis where managers can be effective in rapidly changing markets—where they can react to change, sometimes anticipate it, and occasionally even set the pace of change. Therefore, competing on the edge is at the heart of a winning entrepreneurial strategy.

The second purpose of the chapter is to describe the implementation of competing on the edge. Here our argument is that although managers of new ventures and those leading established corporations share the same strategic destination, they will typically approach "the edge" from two very different starting positions—inflexible and locked into the past in the case of established firms and incoherently chaotic and focused on the future in the case of new ventures. Therefore, the managers in these two kinds of firms will probably travel two very different implementation paths.

We begin by describing "competing on the edge" strategy, the "edges" of chaos and time, and the six key processes that characterize firms whose managers compete on the edge. We then turn to implementing competing on the edge. Here we focus on both the common order of implementation and the distinctive features that are involved in establishing this strategic approach in both new ventures and established corporations. We conclude with a summary of our thinking on entrepreneurial strategy as competing on the edge.

COMPETING ON THE EDGE

Competing on the edge is an approach to strategy in high-velocity and intensely competitive markets. It was developed from in-depth field research in 12 businesses in the global computing industry, an industry in which managing in rapid change is critical for managers in both established firms and new ventures.

The study consisted of six pairs of businesses, with each pair facing a distinct strategic challenge, such as driving leading-edge technology, making difficult trade-offs among price and features, waging standards battles, timing the transition into new computing paradigms, or managing high growth. Each pair consisted of a business that was widely recognized as dominant in its segment of the computer industry, one that was very good but not extraordinary. This business unit level of analysis is particularly important to our thinking in this chapter because this is the level of analysis in established corporations that is most closely related to new ventures.

The first and second authors induced the ideas of competing on the edge from these field data and then sharpened them with insights from complexity theory, the nature of speed, and time-paced evolution (Brown & Eisenhardt, 1998). The result was an approach to strategy that is fundamentally entrepreneurial, given its focus on high-velocity and hotly competitive markets where innovation and change reign.

STRATEGIC SYNTHESIS

Competing on the edge is an approach to entrepreneurial strategy shared by managers in both new ventures and established organizations. Figure 3.1 depicts the strategic synthesis of the established firm and the new venture. Each type of firm is moving in the opposite direction toward a common destination, where a strategy of competing on the edge can be implemented to satisfy the competitive demands of both established firms and new ventures.

Figure 3.1. The Strategic Synthesis of Competing on the Edge

Over the last decade, corporations have tried to renew themselves through downsizing and reengineering. The goal of these efforts has been to create lean, agile, adaptive, and flexible organizations. Layers of management are removed to weaken the bureaucratic structure and to encourage risk taking and innovation. In essence, the bureaucracy wants to be more entrepreneurial.

The new venture wants to remain entrepreneurial; however, with growth comes added structure. Product offerings increase, new markets are entered, and additional staff resources are required. With time, the new venture becomes departmentalized by product, market, or function, and additional employees are hired to manage the growth. Growth continues, and the struggle to fight the transitions from an entrepreneurial firm to a professionally managed organization ensues. Creativity may dissipate and autonomy can weaken as more controls are put in place. In sum, the entrepreneurial firm is fighting the "bureaucratic trap" (Brown & Eisenhardt, 1998).

TWIN BALANCING ACTS

Competing on the edge is a *structural* balancing act (see Figure 3.2). On one side of the scale is the well-developed structure often characteristic of bureaucratic organizations. Bureaucracy emphasizes structure, tight control, and risk aversion regardless of environmental uncertainty (Ross & Unwalla, 1986). The lack of flexibility and the inability to adapt quickly to changes in the competitive environment can often be the demise of these organizations. The stability, size, and structure often associated with the bureaucratic organization also create resistance to change (Kelly & Amburgey, 1991).

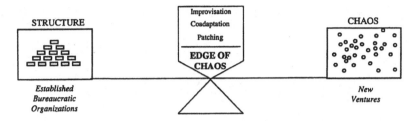

Figure 3.2. The Structural Balancing Act of Competing on the Edge

On the opposite side of the scale lies chaos, which is the prototypical state of organization in many emerging new ventures where few structures and processes are in place. In this type of firm, managers often find themselves going in many directions, trying to seize multiple opportunities, overcome staffing and financial problems, establish a presence in the marketplace, and keep afloat or manage greater-than-expected growth.

Neither side of the scale is the optimal place to operate when competing in the continuously shifting states of disequilibrium that characterize the new competitive landscape. On the one hand, rigid structure creates an organization that cannot easily adapt to change. On the other hand, a chaotic organization with little or no structure does not have the mechanisms in place to effectively coordinate change. As a result, the ideal position lies in the middle at the so-called "edge of chaos."

Competing on the edge is also a *temporal* balancing act (see Figure 3.3). One side of the scale is the orientation toward the past that is typical of established firms. These firms have often experienced past success, and their structures and processes reflect that success in the path-dependent processes that lock history into contemporary organization. Although this emphasis on the past can be an advantage that saves time and lowers risk, it also can be a straightjacket that blocks flexibility in facing new conditions for which past solutions are obsolete.

At the other end of the scale is an orientation toward the future that is typical of new ventures. Many of these companies are founded by people who are focused on the need to escape the past and to grab a place in the exciting future that is unfolding. In these kinds of companies, what is new is what is best. With a mesmerizing future, there is often a profound lack of interest in learning the lessons of the past.

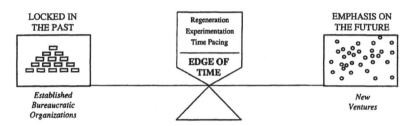

Figure 3.3. The Temporal Balancing Act of Competing on the Edge

As in the case of the edge of chaos, neither extreme of time is the optimal point when competing in markets that are often in disequilibrium. An emphasis on the past creates organizations that cannot move forward. An emphasis on the future creates organizations that flounder in a flood of mistakes. The ideal position is at the middle, along the so-called "edge of time," where managers balance the past and future and manage the pace of evolution between them.

Figures 3.2 and 3.3 represent the balancing acts of the edges of chaos and time, and the six processes involved: (a) improvisation, (b) coadaptation, (c) patching, (d) regeneration, (e) experimentation, and (f) time pacing. Our argument is that incorporating these components into the strategic framework of the organization can make entrepreneurship become standard strategic practice.

EDGE OF CHAOS

The edge of chaos as an entrepreneurial strategy looks quite different from the rational, deliberate prescriptions that fill many strategy textbooks (Russell & Russell, 1992). The traditional management practices of leading, controlling, planning, and directing are very distant from management practices that are unpredictable, diverse, proactive, and even inefficient within firms at the edge of chaos (Brown & Eisenhardt, 1998).

KEY STRUCTURAL PROCESSES

Improvisation refers to operating very flexibly within the constraints of minimum structure or rules. Improvisational theater and jazz have been used as powerful metaphors to illustrate the importance of practicing this concept in organizations (Brown & Eisenhardt, 1998; Crossan, White, Lane, & Klus, 1996). For example, in traditional theater, there is planning and a script. When the play is performed according to plan, the performance is considered successful. Improvisational theater, however, adapts to the audience, and the performance constantly changes. There is no script, and actors are free to develop their role as the performance progresses. "The audience fuels the actors" (Crossan et al., 1996, p. 25), just as market dynamism fuels managers competing at the edge of chaos.

Examining improvisation in jazz provides further insight. Jazz requires the mastery of traditional and basic music skills. When the traditional skills are combined with improvisational skills, innovation is more likely to take place (Crossan et al., 1996). The combination of musical skills and a few organizing rules plus flexibility and real-time communication creates innovative and yet effective music on the stage. Within firms, improvisation suggests that employees must have strong basic skills, operate within minimum structures, and engage in frequent, real-time communication. Only then can firms be adaptive to shifting markets.

The second structural process is *coadaptation*. At the core of coadaptation is collaboration among business units or team members. Even though managers need autonomy to address the unique characteristics of their own business, collaboration is also important so that the sum of the business units will be greater than its parts. In other words, each business is unique, yet capturing the synergy of being a part of the corporation determines success as well.

The third structural process is *patching*. *Patching* refers to the fluid realignment of businesses to market opportunities. Without a patching process, firms tend to remain fixed in dated alignment with markets. In other words, as markets change and opportunities emerge, managers must remain aware of the changes and the "holes" that form in their respective organizations from the market shifts. It is the manager's responsibility to "patch" the holes and realign business activities to match the market.

EDGE OF TIME

The "edge of time" also looks quite different from the typical recipes for success in strategy textbooks. It is distant from core competence perspectives that emphasize building on the past along rigid lines of presumed strategic advantage. It is also distant from the precepts of strategic planning, especially those around the annual planning ritual that occupies many managers. Rather, the "edge of time" rests on a set of temporal processes that emphasize the rhythmic flow of change over time—from past into the present and on to the future.

KEY TEMPORAL PROCESSES

Regeneration is a temporal process that is concerned with combining the old and the new. It recognizes that building on the past is critical for creating competitive advantage because it saves time, saves money, and is often less risky. But regeneration also means avoiding a lock-in with a cash cow product or service forever. Rather, the goal is to find a balance of old opportunities that are often very profitable and comfortable with new, often risky and yet higher-returning opportunities. The result is typically not revolutionary change. Rather, regeneration creates a flow of incremental changes. The process of blending the old with the new spurs managers to make adjustments to the old (e.g., adding new features to an existing product, entering new markets, trying new channels), which in turn allow firms to regenerate and so move into new competitive spaces.

The Walkman product of Sony Corporation is an excellent illustration of regeneration. Sony's strategy was neither to develop the Walkman and then move on to entirely new innovations or technologies nor simply to create a single product that never changed. Rather, the Sony managers regenerated the Walkman business over many years. For example, they first introduced the Walkman as only an AM/FM radio; then they created a Walkman with a cassette, then a waterproof Walkman, and then a sport Walkman. They switched geographies as well. This regeneration of the Walkman business has continued for almost two decades. As a result, Sony managers blended the past with the future to create a continuously regenerated product line and business that gave the company a continuing series of competitive advantages (Barney, 1997).

Given the inherent uncertainty of the future, managers who poise at the "edge of time" also engage in a process of *experimentation*. "Experimentation involves balancing attempts to gain insight into the future that may unfold without losing flexibility to react to the future that does unfold" (Brown & Eisenhardt, 1998, p. 131). At the core of experimentation is developing a wide variety of low-cost probes such as experimental products, market-making alliances, scenario planning sessions, and futurists. The resources spent on these probes, even ones that fail, such as a poor experimental product or a failed prediction, are minimal when compared with those required for entering a new market with a full product rollout that may well fail or with those required to catch up with market leaders who create the future.

The final temporal process is *time pacing*. The norm in many firms is event pacing. That is, an event occurs such as a competitor's introduction of a new product, a government regulation change, or customers' requests for a new feature, and then firm managers act in response to that event (Brown & Eisenhardt, 1998). Often the result of event pacing is that managers find themselves in a constant game of catch-up. Unfortunately, playing catch-up in continuous states of disequilibrium often means "game over" because it is so difficult to get back in the lead when change is rapid (Eisenhardt, 1989).

In contrast, with time pacing, change is not reactively triggered by events but rather proactively triggered at predetermined transition points by managers. People within the firm then find themselves pulsating to predictable rhythms of change (Brown & Eisenhardt, 1997). For example, managers who time-pace might introduce a new product every 14 months, enter five strategic alliances per year, generate 20% of revenue from products introduced in the past 4 years, or open 10 new stores per year. Time-paced transition adds the minimum structure necessary to encourage continuous innovation, allows for constant reassessment of the consequences of an organization's actions in its industry, and "helps managers avert the danger of changing too infrequently" (Brown & Eisenhardt, 1998, p. 67).

IMPLEMENTATION

Implementing an entrepreneurial strategy of competing on the edge is not an easy task. Of course, if it were, then everyone would be doing it. But there are several key ideas to remember. One is that organizations that can change are closer to living organisms than to machines, so implementation is a growth, not an assembly, process. The other is that the starting position of the firm matters for the specifics of the implementation. For new ventures, that position is usually chaotic and obsessed with the future. For established corporations, even those that have downsized and reengineered, the starting position is typically highly structured and locked into the past.

For both kinds of firms, the first step is to get to the *edge of chaos*. For established firms, this typically means a fresh organizational culture that values change and sees it as an opportunity, not a threat. Training in dramatic improvisation is one way to help people to become more entrepreneurial in their thinking and to trigger a culture of change. Getting to the edge of chaos also involves simplification of processes and elimination of structures such as extensive review gates in product development. Although many managers have begun this process through downsizing and reengineering, they often need to eliminate more structure because the goal is agility, not just efficiency. Surprisingly, though, finding the edge of chaos may also involve adding some critical, new structures, including priorities for key operating processes, some real-time measures of operations, and two or three key outcome measures that are clearly assigned to particular individuals. The goal is small and focused business units that are minimally structured and characterized by extensive within- and across-business communication.

For new ventures, finding the edge of chaos often involves adding discipline. Here too, dramatic improvisation can work, but the lesson for employees within new ventures is that a few rules actually permit greater creativity. In these firms, channeling energy into productive directions is often the key to getting to the edge of chaos. This means adding, not eliminating, structures. Here the addition of priority structures on key processes, a few outcome measures, and structured opportunities for communication is critical.

Once managers have maneuvered onto the edge of chaos, they can begin to move to the *edge of time*. For managers within established firms, this often begins with an inventory of capabilities and a switch to modular thinking. One mind-expanding heuristic is to arrange firm capabilities (all significant capabilities, not just core ones) into a "genetic sequence" and then to try different mutations and recombinations to stimulate thinking about new opportunities. In addition to loosening up the past, it is also important to begin thinking more frequently about the future. Future thinking should not be confined to once-a-year planning but rather should be frequent and related to low-cost probes.

For managers within new ventures, the key is to begin to think about the value of experience. Here a mind-expanding heuristic is to think about what the firm's employees really need to do that is new and what can simply be borrowed from the past. The other task is to develop a better insight into the future. As in the case of established firms, the implementation of a low-cost probing strategy is key. For both types of firms, the goal is a flow of strategic moves over time.

The final implementation step is *time pacing*. For established firms, this requires checking for unrecognized rhythms that may be in the organization—the annual budgeting cycle is an obvious one. New ventures should check as well for these rhythms, although their presence is usually minimal. In both types of businesses, managers should also examine competitors, complementors, buyers, and suppliers to learn their rhythms. Then, as in basketball, begin to set rhythms that are advantageous to the firm. Time pacing, together with the edge-of-chaos and edge-of-time processes, creates a "competing on the edge" strategy— "an unpredictable, uncontrollable, and even inefficient strategy that nonetheless . . . works" (Brown & Eisenhardt, 1998, p. 4).

CONCLUSION

When disequilibrium is the norm rather than a rare occurrence, managers in both classic "entrepreneurial" firms and established corporations can gain strategic advantage by being entrepreneurs. This means developing strategies that proactively manage change, build opportunities from that change, and encourage the continuous creation of fresh competitive advantages. Playing a leadership or at least an anticipatory role will position the firm for continuous reinvention, allow for flexibility, and instill change as a natural and even rhythmic occurrence that is inherent in the corporate culture. In contrast, managers who just react to change— whether rigidly or chaotically—lead firms that are destined to decline or even die.

The underlying point of this chapter is that a strategic synthesis is occurring in the new competitive landscape around the entrepreneurial strategy of competing on the edge. This strategy requires managers in all kinds of firms to play an entrepreneurial role. Although the implementation path often differs for managers in new ventures versus those in established corporations, the order (edge of chaos, edge of time, time pacing), the goal (a continuous flow of competitive advantages), and the success metrics (reinvention, growth, and market dominance) are the same. Overall, in markets characterized by disequilibrium, the antecedents to successful firm performance lie in the essence of entrepreneurial strategy—that is, in competing on the edge. As John F. Kennedy stated, "Change is the law of life, and those who look only to the past or the present are certain to miss the future."

REFERENCES

Barney, J. B. (1997). *Gaining and sustaining competitive advantage*. Reading, MA: Addison-Wesley.

Bettis, R. A., & Hitt, M. A. (1995). The new competitive landscape. *Strategic Management Journal, 16*, 7-19.

Brown, S. L., & Eisenhardt, K. M. (1997). The art of continuous change: Linking complexity theory and time-paced evolution in relentlessly shifting organizations. *Administrative Science Quarterly, 42*(1), 1-34.

Brown, S. L., & Eisenhardt, K. M. (1998). *Competing on the edge: Strategy as structured chaos*. Boston: Harvard Business School Press.

Bygrave, W. D. (1989). The entrepreneurship paradigm II: Chaos and catastrophes among quantum jumps? *Entrepreneurship Theory and Practice, 14*(2), 7-29.

Collins, J. C., & Porras, J. I. (1994). *Built to last: Successful habits of visionary companies*. New York: Harper Business.

Crossan, M. M., White, R. E., Lane, H. W., & Klus, L. (1996). The improvising organization: Where planning meets opportunity. *Organizational Dynamics, 24*(4), 20-35.

Eisenhardt, K. M. (1989). Making fast strategic decisions in high-velocity environments. *Academy of Management Journal, 32*, 543-576.

Jacobson, R. (1992). The "Austrian" school of strategy. *Academy of Management Review, 17*, 782-807.

Kelly, D., & Amburgey, T. L. (1991). Organizational inertia and momentum: A dynamic model of strategic change. *Academy of Management Journal, 34*, 591-612.

Price Waterhouse Change Integration Team. (1996). *The paradox principles: How high performance companies manage chaos, complexity, and contradiction to achieve superior results*. Chicago: D. Irwin.

Ross, J., & Unwalla, D. (1986, December). Who is an intrapreneur? *Personnel*, pp. 45-49.

Russell, R. D., & Russell, C. J. (1992). An examination of the effects of organizational norms, organizational structure, and environmental uncertainty on entrepreneurial strategy. *Journal of Management, 18*, 639-656.

Schumpeter, J. A. (1934). *The theory of economic development*. Cambridge, MA: Harvard University Press.

Stacey, R. D. (1996). *Complexity and creativity in organizations*. San Francisco: Berrett-Koehler.

4 | Entrepreneurial Capabilities

A Resource-Based View

Sharon Alvarez
Jay Barney

Strategic management is a process that deals with the entrepreneurial work of the organization, with organizational renewal and growth, and more particularly, with developing and utilizing the strategy which is to guide the organization's operations.

Schendel & Hofer (1978, p. 11)

Strategic managers and researchers have long been interested in understanding sources of organizational renewal, growth, and competitive advantage for firms. An important aspect that should not be overlooked with respect to growth and competitive advantage is innovation and the driver of innovation, entrepreneurship. Entrepreneurship and innovation are inextricably interwoven. But typically, strategic management research that has relied heavily on economic-driven models has overlooked entrepreneurial strategies and entrepreneurial capabilities such as creativity, ingenuity, and foresight. Even today, when entrepreneurship research is in demand, most economic research, and consequently much of strategic management research, views entrepreneurship as the "specter which haunts economic models" (Baumol, 1995, p. 17). Furthermore, the behavioral approach to entrepreneurship has proved to be perhaps even more disappointing than the economic approach. Vesper (1980) found 11 different types of entrepreneurs, and Gartner (1985) classified 8 different types of entrepreneurs. But both of these studies, like most behavioral studies of entrepreneurship, are descriptive and do not move the field closer toward a theory of entrepreneurship (Low & MacMillan, 1988).

Successful firms that over time have demonstrated a sustainable competitive advantage tend to be firms with entrepreneurial vision and strategies. Entrepreneurial vision and strategy are of particular importance to the study of firm competition because firms with entrepreneurial abilities are the ones capable of providing a mechanism for renewal and growth (Schendel & Hofer, 1978). Entrepreneurial ventures can be classified as having three stages. The first stage, pre-entrepreneurship, involves entrepreneurial intentions and entrepreneurial insight. The second stage is the start-up of a new venture and the issues associated with start-up, such as financing. The third stage is firm growth and the sustainability of that growth.

ENTREPRENEURSHIP AND THEORY

Entrepreneurship is a field that offers many insights concerning innovation. However, along with all the promise offered by entrepreneurship studies come profound intellectual problems (Venkataraman, 1997). The first and most significant problem is the lack of a well-articulated, underlying theory of entrepreneurship. A fundamental issue that may underlie the inability to develop entrepreneurship theory is that the necessary and conditional assumptions of entrepreneurship are at best difficult to model in economic terms. As Rumelt (1987) pointed out, "If it can be modeled, it is too late to make money" (p. 156). Behavioral models also have thus far proved disappointing. As Low and MacMillan (1988) stated, "These studies make interesting reading . . . , but it is questionable whether they move us closer toward a theory of entrepreneurship" (p. 148). The lack of supporting theory in entrepreneurship pushes most researchers, particularly strategy researchers, away from using the "e-word."

Still, as recently as 1995, Schendel (1995) called for "more attention to the role of innovation, how it can be managed, and how it can be used to reconfigure competitive advantage in the firm's favor" (p. 181). Schendel placed an emphasis on innovation because he argued that when a competitive advantage is established and sustainable, only innovation can upset the established competitive advantage. He further posited that innovation is "change" in several possible different areas. What we posit is that innovation may be understood through the lens of entrepreneurship.

This chapter suggests reasons why entrepreneurship does not necessarily fit formal theoretical economic analysis and further distances entrepreneurship from past behavioral models. We suggest that as a result of past shortcomings in understanding entrepreneurship, the phenomenon has been left on the sidelines by most current strategic research. We also set out to examine Austrian economic theory, a popular alternative economic theory to entrepreneurship, noting theoretical contributions of this approach. Finally, we offer a resource-based view of entrepreneurship as a theory that may offer insights into entrepreneurship, particularly what we have identified as Stage 3, entrepreneurial firm growth.

ECONOMIC VIEWS
AND ENTREPRENEURSHIP

There are some basic reasons why most economic views have failed to address entrepreneurship. First, traditional neoclassic economic theory treats entrepreneurship as a "mystical" element in enterprise formation (Schendel & Hofer, 1978). Second, entrepreneurship delivers external shocks to the state of equilibrium. The external shocks delivered by entrepreneurial innovation are particularly troublesome within a neoclassical economic view. Neoclassical economics has been traditionally limited with regard to the study of firms because it seldom accounts for organizations' endogenous treatment of technological change (Nelson & Winter, 1982) or changing consumer tastes (Rumelt, Schendel, & Teece, 1991, chap. 1). The lack of emphasis on innovation, heterogeneity, and technological change makes most economic theory that is applied to strategy limited when addressing entrepreneurial strategies. Therefore, although equilibrium is a starting point in understanding the current state of affairs, modeling must go beyond the equilibrium and capture the shocks in the system brought on by innovation (Schumpeter, 1934). Equilibrium assumptions should be relaxed so as not to drive out consideration of innovation, change, and firm heterogeneity. However, it is important to note that formal modeling of innovative shocks to the system and the development of coherent theory are exceedingly difficult (Teece, 1990).

Innovation and entrepreneurship are complex, and an explanation of the phenomena should go beyond most formal economic models. As illustrated by Lippman and Rumelt (1982), considerable uncertainty can be connected with innovation, and new entrants (entrepreneurs) can produce different firm outcomes even when initial endowments are equivalent:

> If the original uncertainty stems from a basic ambiguity concerning the nature of the causal connections between actions and results, the factors responsible for performance differentials will resist precise identification. Under such conditions the uncertainty attaching to entry and imitative attempts persists and complete homogeneity is unattainable. (p. 418)

This argument strongly supports the existence, within firms in an industry, of entrepreneurial differences that may account for heterogeneous performance and immobile assets.

HETEROGENEITY AND ENTREPRENEURSHIP

Hayek (1945) posited an elusive resource that he referred to as day-to-day knowledge. Day-to-day knowledge is typically idiosyncratic because it comes from insights that individuals might gain from their occupation, job routines, networks, and life experiences (Venkataraman, 1997). The uneven distribution of day-to-day knowledge when applied to firm competition can lead to ambiguity and uncertainty, resulting in a competitive advantage. Furthermore, no two individuals will have the same interpretation of their world, thus creating more ambiguity. Entrepreneurs typically act on their day-to-day knowledge when starting firms, exploiting differences of information and causing shocks to an industry.

The concept of day-to-day knowledge has not been extended in the entrepreneurship literature to include entrepreneurial firm growth. However, day-to-day knowledge is of tremendous importance during firm growth. When day-to-day knowledge defies imitation, it can lead to a sustainable competitive advantage, possibly producing supranormal returns or entrepreneurial rents.

Today, a significant portion of strategic research remains static and unable to capture that "mystical element" that may generate entrepreneurial rents. Several respected strategy researchers (Rumelt et al., 1991) have suggested capturing a more dynamic view of strategy with the use of equilibrium economic models that are modified to relax economic assumptions, thus stressing the tendency toward equilibrium. Relaxing equilibrium assumptions of causal ambiguity, known demand, homogeneous returns, and stable technology becomes particularly important when considering the process of innovation and entrepreneurship (Lippman & Rumelt, 1982). The importance of technological innovation and heterogeneity is paramount during entrepreneurial firm growth.

AUSTRIAN ECONOMICS AND ENTREPRENEURSHIP

In much of the entrepreneurship literature, Austrian economics and its applications have been extolled as having considerable potential to enhance strategic thinking and research (Jacobson, 1992). Austrian economics is most widely used when referring to dynamic systems such as those found in entrepreneurial environments. Austrian theory is a disequilibrium perspective, and this theory maintains that entrepreneurs, through innovation, move markets closer to equilibrium. The Austrians view entrepreneurs as a vehicle for promoting discovery and for realizing opportunities in a constantly changing (disequilibrium) marketplace (von Mises, 1949).

What the Austrian view suggests is that empirically modeling business performance to find systematic strategies that firms can implement to earn supranormal returns will be largely unsuccessful. The Austrian view takes into account asymmetric information and entrepreneurial alertness (Kirzner, 1997). In other words, because of differences in information, there is a "gap" in the system that an entrepreneur discovers and exploits, thereby earning entrepreneurial rents. The Austrian view would seem particularly applicable to the study of entrepreneurship. However, the Austrian view proves difficult to apply because of the core assumption that disequilibrium cannot be modeled. The inability to model disequilibrium leaves Austrian theory with little predictive ability, a necessary condition of good theory. Further, the Austrian view does not deal with the sustainability of innovation, an important aspect in entrepreneurial firm growth.

SCHUMPETER
AND ENTREPRENEURSHIP

In times of uncertainty, rapid innovation, and change, the economic competitive model should be a starting place to address innovation and entrepreneurship. Schumpeter's (1934) economic model, which assumes equilibrium until the entrepreneur "shocks" that equilibrium, is perhaps one of the most useful theories in the study of entrepreneurship. In addition, Schumpeter's theory of a disrupted equilibrium may link entrepreneurship to a dynamic study of strategy. As Rumelt (1984) noted, "Business policy research is most closely associated with Schumpeter's vision of competition as the process of creative destruction rather than a static equilibrium condition" (p. 560).

The strong premise of entrepreneurship (Venkataraman, 1997) is based on the disruption of market equilibrium. What this premise holds is that because of human enterprise and advancing knowledge and technology, entrepreneurs will invent equilibrium-destroying innovations in the pursuit of profits. This view of the entrepreneur as an innovator who transforms inventions and ideas into economically viable entities is distinctly Schumpeterian (Baumol, 1995). The Schumpeterian strong premise of entrepreneurship is applicable to the resource-based view of the firm. The innovating entrepreneur is the one who produces constant discovery in terms of products and firm efficiency. The role of the innovating entrepreneur is difficult to describe and analyze systematically and is absent from the standard models of the firm (Baumol, 1995). Because of the ambiguity surrounding the innovating entrepreneur, the entrepreneurial capability of innovation is difficult to imitate. The ambiguity and lack of understanding associated with entrepreneurship and innovation lead to tacit immobile assets and are of particular interest within the resource-based view of the firm.

CURRENT ENTREPRENEURSHIP RESEARCH

Within the field of entrepreneurship, there is a stream of literature that does focus on entrepreneurship as a strategy. However, this approach has been concerned primarily with success factors that enhance the chances of survival. Most literature regarding entrepreneurial success has focused on survival or failure of firms, venture capital acquisition, or start-up firms (Cooper, Woo, & Dunkelberg, 1988; De Castro, Alvarez, & Blasick, 1997; Reynolds, 1987; Vesper, 1982). Understanding the reasons for success or failure of an entrepreneurial firm is important. Still, it is equally important to have guiding theory to help firms identify resources that will take them beyond the start-up phase and into a viable enterprise with the potential for growth.

Entrepreneurial firm resources are often a double-edged sword. Resources that are positive during the start-up phase of the firm may become dysfunctional once survival has been established and the growth phase has begun. An example is decision making. Agile decision making may be good in the initial days of the firm in that many choices have to be made quickly. However, decision-making techniques may have to be altered as the firm becomes more established or additional employees are added. A resource-based view of the firm would be helpful in this situation because it would assist the firm in understanding its key entrepreneurial capabilities and recognizing when these capabilities are no longer functional (West & De Castro, 1998). Understanding entrepreneurial capabilities and how these capabilities interact could help small firms cross the bridge from start-up to growth.

As the literature in entrepreneurship develops, it is important to take inventory of the work that has previously been done. There are still two voids not addressed in the entrepreneurship literature. Today, most of the entrepreneurship literature continues to lack theory (Amit & Schoemaker, 1993; Sandberg, 1992), and what theory is available does not help the entrepreneurial firm exploit its capabilities to enable future innovation and growth.

RESOURCE-BASED THEORY

The resource-based view of competitive advantage examines the link between a firm's internal characteristics and performance and assumes firm heterogeneity and immobility as possible sources of competitive advantage (Barney, 1991; Penrose, 1959; Rumelt, 1984; Wernerfelt, 1984). The concept of firm heterogeneity is perhaps the most common ground between resource-based theory and entrepreneurship in that a central question in entrepreneurship is: Where do opportunities to create goods and services come from? Certainly, one answer is through inventions and discoveries that produce new knowledge.

The resource-based view of firm competition may offer much to the field of entrepreneurship in terms of theoretical development. The resource-based view emphasizes firm resource heterogeneity and immobility as possible sources of competitive advantage (Barney, 1991; Conner, 1991; Penrose, 1959; Rumelt, 1984; Wernerfelt, 1984). However, what makes firm resources heterogeneous or immobile is what makes the study of entrepreneurship so difficult. If competitors know exactly what resources make a firm successful, the resource can be imitated. In the same vein, if competitors know what the factors of production are, then these factors can become mobile (Lippman & Rumelt, 1982). If entrepreneurial capabilities are known, then they cease to be entrepreneurial.

Resource heterogeneity and immobility are the cornerstones of entrepreneurial success because firm heterogeneity may well be a result of entrepreneurial capabilities. The strong premise of entrepreneurship particularly coincides with the notions of resource heterogeneity. The strong premise assumption is that as markets approach equilibrium, the lure of profits, advancing knowledge, and technology will shock the equilibrium (Schumpeter, 1934; Venkataraman, 1997). When an entrepreneurial innovation shocks the equilibrium, a firm will have a competitive advantage until the Schumpeterian "swarms" are able to imitate the innovation. When a firm can consistently maintain entrepreneurial innovations, it will keep its competitors in a constant game of "catch-up," never becoming quite able to imitate the original firm. The firm that can consistently use its entrepreneurial capabilities to innovate may have a sustained competitive advantage.

Conner (1991) has addressed the unexplored issue of entrepreneurship within resource-based theory and opened the door for further exploration by stating that "in a resource-based view, discerning appropriate inputs is ultimately a matter of entrepreneurial vision and intuition; the creative act underlying such vision is a subject that so far has not been a central focus of resource-based theory development" (p. 134). Although it is true that little work in resource-based theory has incorporated entrepreneurship explicitly, Conner compared Schumpeter's work to resource- based theory, pointing out that both theories rest on the following assumptions:

- Spectacular above-normal returns can result from new ways of competing.
- Entrepreneurial vision is at the heart of the firm.
- Potential imitators always exist.

Entrepreneurial strategies and capabilities such as agile and flexible decision making, creativity, ingenuity, and foresight are essentially resource assets that are inimitable by definition. Entrepreneurial assets within the resource-based view of the firm are resource bundles, or what Schumpeter called "new combinations," and are often unique, idiosyncratic, and sometimes unknown to the firm itself.

We posit that resource-based theory can include entrepreneurship within its framework. Entrepreneurial capabilities such as agility, creativity, and fast decision making are causally ambiguous and many times inimitable. The persistence of entrepreneurial capabilities over time can lead to a sustained competitive advantage.

Entrepreneurial firms, perhaps more than any other type of firm, rely on idiosyncratic firm attributes to maintain a competitive position. Entrepreneurial firms are often born because they control different strategically relevant resources or employ the resources they do possess in strategically different ways from the industry norms. Second, because these firms are often the new players, entrepreneurial firms usually are the more heterogeneous firms.

RESOURCE-BASED THEORY
AND ENTREPRENEURSHIP

Lippman and Rumelt (1982) noted that "considerable uncertainty connected with major commercial ventures and de novo entry will produce a dispersion in the results obtained by different firms even when initial endowments are equivalent" (p. 418). In a purely economic equilibrium model, the dispersion produced will be eliminated when initial endowments are equal. Schumpeter (1934) also posited that the time between an innovation and imitation would last only as long as it took for the "swarms" to imitate the entrepreneur. Yet obviously some firms outperform other firms over a considerable length of time. Sometimes there is not a clear reason why these firms outperform other firms, and sometimes the answer lies in the longevity of the firm. However, the answer is just as likely to be that firms with a sustained advantage also have sustained innovation that is difficult to copy. Herein lies the problem of entrepreneurship research. There is an ambiguity surrounding causal connections between actions and results (Lippman & Rumelt, 1982), an ambiguity that is the essence of entrepreneurship. If the ambiguity surrounding entrepreneurial innovations is difficult for competitors to copy, it is even more problematic to model and theorize.

In this chapter, the juncture where discovery and innovation meet is termed the entrepreneurial advantage (Figure 4.1). The entrepreneurial advantage is the result of employing entrepreneurial assets to create entrepreneurial rents.

ENTREPRENEURIAL
ADVANTAGE

A sustained competitive advantage can disrupt the equilibrium because innovation is often used to maintain that advantage, and innovation can disrupt a sustained advantage. Because entrepreneurship is often the driver of innovation, a viewpoint of strategy that incorporates entrepreneurship and entrepreneurial capabilities is suggested. Entrepreneurial capabilities are by definition unique, inimitable, valuable, rare assets.

Rumelt (1987) recommended that more of an emphasis be placed on the uniqueness of firms and that profit be identified "with resource bundles rather than with collectives" (p. 140). He extended his argument to include entrepreneurial rents that accrue as a result of entrepreneurship. His definition of entrepreneurship is similar to Schumpeter's in that entrepreneurship is the discovery of new combinations of resources

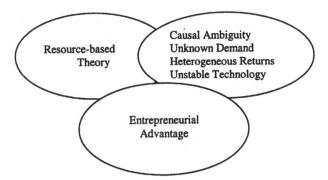

Figure 4.1. Entrepreneurial Advantage

under uncertain situations that generate entrepreneurial rent as a reward for risk taking. As Lippman and Rumelt (1982) noted, "Uncertain imitability obtains when the creation of new production functions is inherently uncertain and when either causal ambiguity or property rights in unique resources impede imitation and factor mobility" (p. 421).

Rumelt (1987) defined entrepreneurial rent as the difference between a venture's ex post value and the ex ante cost of the resources combined to form a venture. If equilibrium is the norm, then there are no entrepreneurial rents because ex ante cost equals ex post value. The entrepreneurial rents are profits that are made when uncertainty or disequilibrium is occurring, and entrepreneurial insight occurs as a result of this uncertainty. In this case, the entrepreneurial insight and day-to-day knowledge are the resource assets that might yield a possible source of sustained competitive advantage. The competitive advantage achieved through entrepreneurship yields an entrepreneurial rent. For example, if a venture is making $5 on a widget that can recover all profits at $3, the difference of $2 is the entrepreneurial rent. Entrepreneurship is the asset that gives the organization the competitive advantage to earn this extra rent.

However, competitors or swarms are watching this entrepreneurial rent, and they quickly try to imitate the product or process that generated it, thereby dissipating the rent. The assumption of a dissipating rent is a main difference between resource-based theory and the Austrian view of entrepreneurship that has gained current popularity. Jacobson (1992) noted that the Austrians view a competitive advantage as dissipating over time whereas resource-based theory views a competitive advantage as sustainable. We suggest that the organization with a sustainable advantage is not one that can sustain any one innovation indefinitely against competitors but instead one that can continue to innovate and stay one innovation ahead of its competitors. Sustainability is the entrepreneurial ability to innovate past the point of imitation, an inimitable entrepreneurial resource. Figure 4.2 is an illustration of the traditional school of thought, in which there is a system tending toward equilibrium that is disrupted by an innovation, and then the system tends back toward equilibrium.

The resource-based view of a sustained advantage allows for continuous innovation, not just a one-time innovation. Thus, the system is more circular in that innovation is a normal part of the system with entrepreneurial assets, such as day-to-day knowledge and information, driving innovation (Figure 4.3). The entrepreneurial assets can be learning, knowledge, and creativity, assets that are often unknown to the firm.

Resource-based theory views learning and knowledge as resources of the organization and considers the ability to innovate as a competitive advantage that leads to profits. Knowledge is typically idiosyncratic because it is acquired in day-to-day activities and individual activities. The acquisition of knowledge through day-to-day activities is considered to have been obtained in a "knowledge corridor" (Kirzner, 1985; Nelson & Winter, 1982) and can lead to entrepreneurial insight, innovation, possible sustained competitive advantage, and ultimately entrepreneurial rent.

FIRM RESOURCES AND
ENTREPRENEURSHIP

Firm resources typically include all assets, capabilities, organizational processes, firm attributes, information, and knowledge controlled by a firm that enable the firm to conceive of and implement strategies that improve its efficiency and effectiveness (Barney, 1991; Daft, 1983). However, firm resources that can be termed entrepreneurial capabilities are for the first time explicitly added to the list of firm resources.

Figure 4.2. Equilibrium and Innovation

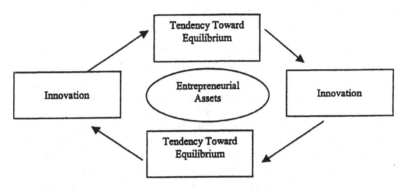

Figure 4.3. Equilibrium and Constant Innovation

A firm is said to have a competitive advantage when it is implementing a value-creating strategy not simultaneously being implemented by any current or potential competitors and when these other firms are unable to duplicate the benefits of this strategy (Barney, 1991). A value-creating strategy not being implemented by any current or potential competitors is an entrepreneurial strategy and thus an entrepreneurial capability. Within this definition, a competitive advantage pertains to both current competitors and also potential competitors that might enter an industry at some future date. However, in contrast to past theories of entrepreneurship such as the Austrian view, entrepreneurial discovery and insight are not isolated events that are dissipated by competitors. Instead, entrepreneurial discovery and insight are intangible entrepreneurial assets that lead to a series of innovations in the pipeline of a firm, giving the firm a possible source of sustained competitive advantage.

A sustained competitive advantage depends on the possibility of overcoming competitive duplication. For example, once a competitive advantage is duplicated, it ceases to be a competitive advantage and therefore is not sustained. In this sense, a sustained competitive advantage is an equilibrium definition (Barney, 1991; Hirshleifer, 1980). However, if one considers the example of Sony, whose competitive advantage is its ability to constantly innovate and stay one innovation ahead of its competitors, the argument can be made that Sony has an entrepreneurial intangible asset whereby innovation is ongoing, a Schumpeterian story of entrepreneurship. Sony uses an entrepreneurial strategy that drives innovation and maintains its competitive advantage.

> Sony possesses special management and coordination skills that enable it to conceive, design, and manufacture high quality miniaturized consumer electronics. However, virtually every time Sony brings out a new miniaturized product, several of its competitors quickly duplicate that product through reverse engineering, thereby reducing Sony's technological advantage. After Sony introduces each new product, it experiences a rapid increase in profits attributable to the new product's unique features. This increase, however, leads other firms to reverse-engineer the Sony product and introduce their own version. Increased competition results in a reduction in profits associated with a new version. Increased competition results in a reduction in profits associated with a new product. (Barney, 1997, pp. 159-160)

Sony's experience could be explained without addressing entrepreneurship as part of the explanation. However, when you consider that Sony's sustained advantage stems from the ability to innovate beyond its competitors' ability to imitate, the notion of an entrepreneurial capability becomes probable. What happens next is consistent with a resource-based view of events that easily incorporates an entrepreneurial capability view.

> At the level of individual products, Sony apparently enjoys only a temporary competitive advantage. However, looking at the total returns earned by Sony across all of its new products over time makes it clear that the source of Sony's sustained competitive advantage is an entrepreneurial asset. By exploiting its resources and capabilities in miniaturization, Sony is able to constantly introduce new and exciting personal electronics products. Over time across several product introductions, Sony's entrepreneurial resources and capability advantages lead to a sustained competitive advantage. (Barney, 1997, pp. 159-160)

The second Sony example illustrates a resource-based view of a sustained competitive advantage. Sony's ability to maintain a sustained competitive advantage depends on the entrepreneurial ability to constantly innovate. A pipeline of entrepreneurial creativity feeds the junction where sustainability and innovation meet.

ENTREPRENEURIAL CREATIVITY AND SUSTAINED INNOVATION

Resource-based theory is consistent with the entrepreneurial perspective that maintains that entrepreneurial discovery and profits are the reasons for innovation. Similar to the current view of entrepreneurship, the resource-based perspective views profits not as a result of monopoly power but as a result of discovery and innovation. We extend the view of entrepreneurship as discovery for profit and thus innovation to include entrepreneurial firm growth.

Entrepreneurial discovery might include product reengineering, a new use for an old product, new manufacturing methods, distribution channels, or the discovery of new ways of competing that competitors have overlooked: in essence, what Schumpeter (1934) called new ways of doing business, "new combinations." These new combinations bring about firm heterogeneity within an industry and may create a competitive advantage. Von Mises (1949) posited that it is the entrepreneur who first sees and understands the gap between what is currently being done and what is possible. Resource-based theory suggests that it may be the entrepreneurial firm that can consistently fill the gaps between what is currently being done and what is possible.

Resource-based theory traditionally has viewed a sustainable competitive advantage within the bounds of equilibrium. However, if we encompass Schumpeter's view of equilibrium shocks caused by entrepreneurial innovations, a series of these shocks could lead the firm perpetuating the shocks to a sustained competitive advantage. Popular theories of entrepreneurship such as the Austrian viewpoint argue that there is no equilibrium, only disequilibrium, which entrepreneurs see and take advantage of by introducing new innovation. Austrians argue that for an economy to be in equilibrium, innovation must decrease and that because competitors imitate strategies known to generate above-normal returns, entrepreneurial rents are only temporary. However, we argue that firms with a sustainable advantage due to innovation fueled by entrepreneurial capabilities such as creativity and insight gained through the "knowledge corridor" need not lose an overall sustainable advantage—a point illustrated in the Sony example.

CONCLUSION

The last two decades have seen a rise in and appreciation for entrepreneurship and entrepreneurs. The academic field of entrepreneurship has gained status as a legitimate scholarly research subject (Stevenson & Jarillo, 1990). The field has its own journals such as *Journal of Business Venturing*, and entrepreneurship articles are accepted in mainstream strategy journals. The importance of entrepreneurship lies in the possibility that firm creation and firm growth can be the drivers of economic growth and thus create thousands of new jobs (Birch, 1979; Birley, 1987; Reynolds, 1987). However, as literature on entrepreneurship has emerged, there are still calls for more theory-driven work (Low & MacMillan, 1988), and some academics still question entrepreneurship's claim to intellectual legitimacy (Venkataraman, 1997).

Timmons (1982) reviewed the entrepreneurship literature and suggested that it had "substantial variations in content, assumptions, and emphasis, and little theory to anchor the variety of viewpoints" (p. 132). Since the Timmons review, research in the field of entrepreneurship has included work identifying firm traits such as growth (Drucker, 1985) and flexibility (Birch, 1979). However, these traits are deemed to be important to all firms, not just to entrepreneurial firms. Further work in this area has consisted of identifying individual entrepreneur behaviors, following the work of March and Simon (1958), but once again, many of the behaviors encountered are not particular to entrepreneurs but could be applicable to managers in larger firms as well. Finally, Gartner (1985) concluded that entrepreneurial firms are too diverse to permit generalization. However, we would suggest not that entrepreneurial firms have been too diverse to permit generalization but that the concentration of theory development has been on the individual entrepreneur and not on the entrepreneurial capabilities of the firm. In other words, as a field, entrepreneurship has been concerned with the entrepreneur and not with the entrepreneurial firm.

A neglected issue in entrepreneurship literature has been a lack of theory explaining entrepreneurial firms. A neglected issue within resource-based theory has been the contribution of entrepreneurial capabilities toward a competitive advantage and, more importantly, toward a possible sustained competitive advantage. However, it can be claimed that the dominant logic common to entrepreneurial firms is the firm's entrepreneurial capabilities, which fuel innovation, giving the firm a possible sustained competitive advantage.

Many entrepreneurial firms are not aware of what their entrepreneurial capabilities might be or do not know that they can incorporate strategies to help them exploit these capabilities. Do firm age and size define an entrepreneurial firm, or is an entrepreneurial firm one such as Sony that acts entrepreneurial in order to innovate and maintain a possible sustained competitive advantage? The answer is probably both. If the answer is both, then strategy researchers should be more careful in incorporating an entrepreneurial view in their framework. Still, this is an area that has been left largely unanswered by most strategic management scholars and entrepreneurship scholars.

REFERENCES

Amit, R., & Schoemaker, P. (1993). Strategic assets and organizational rent. *Strategic Management Journal, 14,* 33-46.

Barney, J. B. (1991). Firm resources and sustained competitive advantage. *Journal of Management, 17,* 99-120.

Barney, J. B. (1997). *Gaining and sustaining competitive advantage.* Reading, MA: Addison-Wesley.

Baumol, W. J. (1995). Formal entrepreneurship theory in economics: Existence and bounds. In I. Bull, H. Thomas, & G. Willard (Eds.), *Entrepreneurship.* Terrytown, NY: Elsevier Science.

Birch, D. L. (1979). *The job generation process.* Cambridge: MIT Program on Neighborhood and Regional Change.

Birley, S. (1987). New ventures and employment growth. *Journal of Business Venturing, 2*(2), 155-165.

Conner, K. R. (1991). A historical comparison of resource-based theory and five schools of thought within industrial organization economics: Do we have a new theory of the firm? *Journal of Management, 17,* 121-154.

Cooper, A., Woo, C., & Dunkelberg, W. (1988). Entrepreneurs' perceived chances for success. *Journal of Business Venturing, 3,* 97-108.

Daft, R. (1983). *Organization theory and design.* New York: West.

DeCastro, J. O., Alvarez, S. A., & Blasick, J. (1997). An examination of the nature of business closings: Are they really failures? In P. D. Reynolds, W. D. Bygrave, N. M. Carter, P. Davidsson, W. Gartner, C. M. Mason, & P. P. McDougall (Eds.), *Frontiers of entrepreneurship research.* Wellesley, MA: Babson College, Center for Entrepreneurial Studies.

Drucker, P. (1985). *Innovation and entrepreneurship: Practice and principles.* New York: Harper & Row.

Gartner, W. B. (1985). A conceptual framework for describing the phenomenon of new venture creation. *Academy of Management Review, 10,* 696-706.

Hayek, F. A. (1945). The use of knowledge in society. *American Economic Review, 35,* 519-530.

Hirshleifer, J. (1980). *Price theory and applications.* Englewood Cliffs, NJ: Prentice Hall.

Jacobson, R. (1992). The Austrian school of strategy. *Academy of Management Review, 17,* 782-805.

Kirzner, I. M. (1985). *Discovery and the capitalist process.* Chicago: University of Chicago Press.

Kirzner, I. M. (1997). *How markets work: Disequilibrium, entrepreneurship and discovery.* Westminster, UK: Institute of Economic Affairs.

Lippman, S. A., & Rumelt, R. P. (1982). Uncertain imitability: An analysis of interfirm differences in efficiency under competition. *Bell Journal of Economics, 13*), 418-438.

Lorenz, C. (1963). Deterministic Nonperiodic Flow. *Journal of the Atmospheric Sciences, 20,* 130-141.

Low, M. B., & MacMillan, I. C. (1988). Entrepreneurship: Past research and future challenges. *Journal of Management, 14*(2), 139-161.

March, J. G., & Simon, A., II. (1958). *Organization.* New York: John Wiley.

Nelson, R., & Winter, S., (1982). *An evolutionary theory of economic change.* Cambridge, MA: Harvard University Press.

Penrose, E. T. (1959). *The growth of the firm.* New York: John Wiley.

Reynolds, P. D. (1987). New firms: Societal contribution versus survival potential. *Journal of Business Venturing, 2,* 231-246.

Rumelt, R. P. (1984). Towards a strategic theory of the firm. In R. B. Lamb (Ed.), *Competitive strategic management* (pp. 556-570). Englewood Cliffs, NJ: Prentice Hall.

Rumelt, R. P. (1987). Theory, strategy, and entrepreneurship. In D. J. Teece (Ed.), *The competitive challenge.* Cambridge, MA: Ballinger.

Rumelt, R. P., Schendel, D. E., & Teece, D. J. (1991). *Fundamental issues in strategy: A research agenda.* Boston: Harvard Business School Press.

Sandberg, W. (1992, Spring). Strategic management's potential contributions to a theory of entrepreneurship. *Entrepreneurship Theory and Practice, 16*(3), 73-90.

Schendel, D. (1995). Strategy futures: What's left to worry about? *Advances in Strategic Management, 11B,* 143-188.

Schendel, D., & Hofer, C. W. (1978). Introduction to the Pittsburgh Conference. In D. E. Schendel & C. W. Hofer (Eds.), *Strategic management: A new view of business policy and planning.* Boston: Little, Brown.

Schumpeter, J. A. (1934). *The theory of economic development.* Cambridge, MA: Harvard University Press.

Stevenson, H. H., & Jarillo, J. C. (1990). A paradigm of entrepreneurial management. *Strategic Management Journal, 11,* 17-27.

Teece, D. J. (1990). Contributions and impediments of economic analysis to the study of strategic management. In J. W. Fredrickson (Ed.), *Perspectives on strategic management* (pp. 39-80). New York: Harper & Row.

Timmons, J. A. (1982). New venture creation: Methods and models. In C. A. Kent, D. L. Sexton, & K. H. Vesper (Eds.), *Encyclopedia of entrepreneurship* (pp. 126-138). Englewood Cliffs, NJ: Prentice Hall.

Venkataraman, S. (1997). The distinctive domain of entrepreneurship research. In J. A. Katz (Ed.), *Advances in entrepreneurship, firm emergence, and growth* (pp. 119-138). Greenwich, CT: JAI.

Vesper, K. H. (1980). *New venture strategies.* Englewood Cliffs, NJ: Prentice Hall.

Vesper, K. H. (1982). Introduction and summary of entrepreneurship research. In C. A. Kent, D. L. Sexton, & K. H. Vesper (Eds.), *Encyclopedia of entrepreneurship.* Englewood Cliffs, NJ: Prentice Hall.

Von Mises, L. (1949). *Human action: A Treatise on economics.* Chicago: Henry Regenry.

Wernerfelt, B. (1984). A resource-based view of the firm. *Strategic Management Journal, 5,* 171-180.

West, P. G., & DeCastro, J. O. (1998). *Achilles' heel: Distinctive inadequacies and resource weaknesses.* Working Paper, University of Colorado at Boulder.

5 | Entrepreneurial Management as Strategy

Raphael H. Amit
Keith Brigham
Gideon D. Markman

Entrepreneurial management is a management system under which organizational members are empowered to think and act like entrepreneurs. This chapter draws on concepts from resource-based theory, institutional theory, organizational processes, learning organization, and dominant logic to explore the potential rewards of embracing such a management system. It is our contention that strategies of entrepreneurial management are essential to firms if they are to develop unique *strategic assets* and *institutional capital*—the foundations of sustainable competitive advantage.

In the new competitive era (Bettis & Hitt, 1995), firms often operate in environments that are turbulent and uncertain. To be effective in these environments, managers must continually develop new tools, concepts, systems, and mind-sets. Flexibility and agility are paramount. Managers must possess an entrepreneurial mind-set that emphasizes innovation and creativity (Bettis & Hitt, 1995). As a result of hypercompetitive pressures, programmed work is becoming more fluid, repetitive tasks are becoming nonrepetitive, tenured positions are being eliminated, and role-based works are forming around knowledge and personnel initiatives (Rousseau,

1997). New employment models (i.e., telecommuting, off-site sales forces, independent contractors) that involve reduced interactions between employees and their managers diminish opportunities for managerial supervision of subordinates. This limited authority and control, coupled with the increase in the number of professional and technical jobs, challenges structures and command lines typically associated with traditional management styles and predictable markets. With fewer external controls on work, greater value is derived from improvisation, curiosity, learning, and, ultimately, innovation (Weick, 1996).

As this chapter will show, entrepreneurial management offers guidance and assistance for firms attempting to successfully traverse this new competitive landscape. In the following section, we use Amit and Schoemaker's (1993) *strategic assets/strategic industry factors* framework to examine how a strategy of entrepreneurial management complements a firm's overall market strategy and competitive posture.

STRATEGIC ASSETS/STRATEGIC INDUSTRY FACTORS FRAMEWORK

The concept of key *success factors* has played an important role in strategic management (Ghemawat, 1991a). However, Amit and Schoemaker (1993) proposed that the notion of key success factors be replaced with *strategic industry factors* at the industry level of analysis and with *strategic assets* at the firm level of analysis. According to the strategic assets/strategic industry factors framework, resources are converted into final products or services through the combination of a variety of assets and "bonding mechanisms" such as technology, information and incentive systems, and credibility and trust among management and labor. Resources in this context consist of internal, tradable *know-hows* (e.g., patents, trademarks, licenses), financial and physical assets (e.g., property, plants, equipment), and human capital (Amit & Schoemaker, 1993).

Capabilities refers to a firm's ability to use organizational processes to marshal its resources and achieve desired objectives. Capabilities are firm-specific, information-based processes that are developed over time through complex interactions among the firm's resources. They can be conceptualized as intermediate goods generated by the firm to provide enhanced productivity of its resources. However, unlike a firm's resources, capabilities are based on the development and transfer of information through the firm's human capital (Amit & Schoemaker, 1993). In addition, the information-based capabilities of a firm (what Itami, 1987, termed *invisible assets*) depend not only on the firm's employees but also on the perceptions held by the firm's customers, suppliers, and competitors. Capabilities are often developed in functional areas or through combining physical, human, and technological resources at the corporate level. Thus, firms may build corporate capabilities including reliable service, repeated processes of product innovations, manufacturing flexibility, increased responsiveness to developing market needs, and short product development cycles (Amit & Schoemaker, 1993).

A portion of a firm's resources, but its capabilities in particular, may be subject to market failure. That is, the market may allocate these factors in an inefficient and imperfect manner. Several sources of market failure have been suggested, including small numbers, opportunism, and information impactedness (Williamson, 1975). Factor specialization in terms of use or location can also result in market failure (Klein, Crawford, & Alchian, 1978). Along the same lines, Caves (1984) highlighted sunk costs and suggested that a factor's value is inversely related to the extent of its specialization for a particular use or industry setting. Therefore, *strategic assets* are sets of scarce, unique, inimitable, idiosyncratic, nontradable, intangible, and nonsubstitutable appropriable and specialized resources and capabilities that generate a firm's competitive advantage (Amit & Schoemaker, 1993; Barney, 1991).

Specific resources and capabilities—*strategic industry factors*—are subject to market failures and are the prime determinants of economic rents within an industry. In fact, industries may be classified in terms of the strategic industry factors that drive competition by virtue of dominating the structure of sunk costs incurred in the course of competition (Ghemawhat, 1991b). Strategic industry factors, in this context, are characterized by their proneness to market failures and subsequent asymmetric distribution over firms. By definition, strategic industry factors are determined at the market level through complex interactions among the firm's competitors, exogenous shocks, customer preferences, regulators, external industry innovations, and other constituencies and stakeholders. The relevant set of strategic industry factors changes over time and cannot be predicted with complete certainty (Schoemaker & Amit, 1994). However, we believe that in the new competitive landscape, the relevant set of strategic industry factors will be more "entrepreneurial" (specific resources and capabilities dependent on pro-active agility, curiosity, learning, and innovation).

The challenge that top management teams face is to identify, ex ante, the set of strategic assets that will establish the firm's sustainable competi-tive advantage and thereby generate exceptional rents. These are eco-nomic rents that stem from the organization's resources and capabilities and that can be appropriated by the organization as an ecosystem (rather than any single factor). This requires managers to identify both present and future sets of strategic industry factors. It also demands that they make decisions on the further development of existing and new strategic assets—those that are most likely to contribute to the creation and protec-tion of economic rents. Not every firm will succeed with its targeted sets of strategic assets, as their applicability and relevance ultimately hinge on the complex interactions and processes referred to above. Examples of possible strategic assets include technological capability, accelerated product-development cycles, brand management, control of or superior access to distribution channels, a cost-effective firm structure, quality and lasting buyer-seller relationships, intensive and consequential R&D ven-tures and capabilities, world-class service, and an impeccable reputation (Schoemaker & Amit, 1994).

As alluded to earlier, the strategic value of a firm's resources and capabili-ties is enhanced when resources are scarce, unique, inimitable, idiosyn-cratic, nontradable, intangible, and nonsubstitutable (Oliver, 1997). For example, invisible assets such as tacit organizational knowledge, human resource practices, or even trust between management and labor are organizational processes that are hard to trade or replicate (by com-petitors) because they are deeply rooted in the organization's implicit and explicit infrastructure. Such process-based assets accumulate over a period of time and eventually become highly firm specific. The focus here is not just on the material aspects of resources and capabilities but mainly on the processes and their transformational characteristics. These are often specific to a firm and/or industry at a given point in time. Such idiosyncrasy makes resources and capabilities difficult to imitate. Further, even when imitation is possible, their development time cannot easily be compressed.

The applicability of a firm's bundle of resources and capabilities to a particular industry setting (i.e., the overlap with the set of strategic indus-try factors) determines the available rents. Managers can influence the development and deployment of strategic assets by adopting a "process" (in contrast to an input-output) perspective. This standpoint recognizes distinct phases of development, the importance of feedback, and the need for corporate vision. It also entails careful scripting of how resources, information, and personnel are combined and sequenced over time to produce specific capabilities.

INSTITUTIONAL THEORY

Scholars have recently called for an organization-based theory of competitive advantage (Barney & Zajac, 1994) and for a theory combining institutional and resource-based perspectives (Oliver, 1997; Rao, 1994). They have argued that, despite providing a valuable framework, the resource-based view draws an incomplete picture of *how* firms attain and sustain competitive advantage. As described in the previous section, the resource-based perspective proposes that sustainable competitive advantage is the result of bounded rational management decisions, the accumulation of strategic assets, strategic industry factors, and imperfect factor markets. Although it is clear that economic factors drive resource allocation, resource-based theory does not tell us *how* firms should make strategic decisions. To address this challenge, then, the following section will build on institutional theory and its view of institutionalized processes and contexts as a source of competitive advantage.

In contrast to resource-based theory, the institutional perspective proposes that decisions are driven by more than economic forces. Rather, judgment and decision making are the result of legitimacy, social justification, and even obligation (Zukin & DiMaggio, 1990). That is, managers and firms operate within a social nexus of norms, values, and assumptions about what is appropriate or socially acceptable behavior (Oliver, 1997). Whereas the resource-based framework focuses on the degree to which firm behavior is rational and economically driven, institutional theory emphasizes the degree to which firm behavior is compliant, habitual, routinized, and socially driven (Oliver, 1997). Institutional theory suggests that the rent-generating ability of a firm's strategic assets depends not only on the fit between the strategic assets and the firm's strategic industry factors but also on the degree of fit between the strategic assets and the political and cultural environment of the firm (Oliver, 1997).

Thus, to achieve a sustainable competitive advantage, a firm must be aware of, and actively manage, its institutionalized processes and contexts.

RESOURCE CAPITAL AND
INSTITUTIONAL CAPITAL

Combining the resource-based and institutional perspectives, Oliver (1997) introduced the concepts of *resource* and *institutional capitals.* Capital is a durable, tangible or intangible resource or capability that contributes to a sustainable competitive advantage. Resource capital is the value-enhancing assets and competencies of the firm. Institutional capital is the firm's ability to support and use its value-enhancing assets and competencies (Oliver, 1997). Whereas resource capital is similar to resources, capabilities, and strategic assets (discussed in the previous section), *institutional capital* refers more to the organizational context that influences how effectively resource capital may be used. Resource and institutional capitals are complementary sources for sustained competitive advantage.

To attain and sustain competitive advantage, firms must maximize their stocks of—or access to—both resource and institutional capitals without acquiring excessive costs that are typically associated with such assets. Oliver (1997) proposed several ideal structural characteristics and resource strategies for firms to build these stocks (see Table 5.1). Structural characteristics may include decentralized structures, incentive systems that reward innovation and continuous improvement, cross-functional teams that enhance learning and knowledge transfer, formalized resource evaluation systems, horizontal information and technology flows, and employee hiring and development systems that stress curiosity, knowledge, and learning. Resource strategies may include continuous monitoring of customer and competitor perceptions about the firm's resources, market-driven resource investments, efforts to reduce turnover of key personnel, attention to employee perceptions or "buy-in," the acquisition and deployment of critical resources, and global benchmarking of core resource practices (Oliver, 1997).

TABLE 5.1 Resource and Institutional Capitals as Sources of Sustainable Competitive Advantage

Key Aspects	Resource Capitals	Institutional Capitals
Definition	Tangible and intangible value-enhancing resources and capabilities	Routines and processes that enhance optimal use of resource capital
Examples	Patents, superb distribution channels; rapid production cycles; cost-effective structures, competencies, and systems; nonappropriable management talent; superior management-employee relations	Culture of continuous improvement; habitual emphasis on resource innovation, learning, problem solving, knowledge sharing, and programs and technologies that accelerate resource adoption
Key success factors	Acquisition and protection of rare, inimitable resources and capabilities	Effective management of judgment and decision making
Ways to enhance capital	Efficient recognition and evaluation of resources, use of interindustry links for resource information and control, rewards and promotional advances for resource champions, horizontal communication flows	Incentive systems tied to resource innovations and competency, investment in resource performance, hiring based on resource expertise, team-based structure
Factors that deplete capital	Security leaks, outsourcing key personnel, emphasis on opportunism and short-term mentality	Stagnant culture, rewarding loyalty to management rather than performance, vested interest in the status quo

SOURCE: Adapted from Oliver (1997).

ENTREPRENEURIAL MANAGEMENT

In contrast to the two theories discussed above, *entrepreneurial management* refers to the firm's internal management systems and organizational processes and the extent to which these enable it to execute its chosen market strategy. It is a management philosophy that promotes strategic agility, flexibility, creativity, and continuous innovation. The primary objective of an entrepreneurial management system is thus to develop incumbents within all levels of an organization who think and act like entrepreneurs. Thus, all employees of a firm keep the overarching goals as well as the benchmark objectives of the entire business in mind. They are also empowered to build their autonomy and accountability by engaging in judgments and decision making that involve calculated risks and by taking responsibility for those outcomes. Entrepreneurial management represents more of a continuous process than an end state. For an organization, having all of its members think and act like entrepreneurs may be unrealistic. In fact, it is suspected that initally—during the incipient phase of such practice—entrepreneurial management could bring a diminishing return due to risk-taking ventures and other personnel activities that were never allowed before. However, it is our conviction that after entrepreneurial management becomes an organization's "second nature," firms will experience above-normal returns. In short, a firm's movement toward entrepreneurial management is realistic and could be of vital strategic importance. Table 5.2 lists some of the characteristic elements in an organization employing entreprencurial management.

INTEGRATIVE EXAMPLE

The following example will illustrate how the concepts introduced thus far generate a sustainable competitive advantage. Suppose a firm employs a *first-mover* strategy. This firm's external market strategy is to continually be the first to market with new and innovative products. In choosing to pursue this particular market strategy, assume that the firm has identified the strategic industry factors for its industry and that these include innovative products, quick response to market trends, and fast product development cycles. Having identified these strategic industry factors and chosen its external market strategy, the firm faces the challenge of developing the strategic assets (the relevant stock of resource capital) and the complementary stock of institutional capital that will optimize the execution of its chosen market strategy. The set of strategic assets needed to implement this strategy should overlap with the strategic industry factors and will thus include the development of internal capabilities such as repeated product innovations, awareness of and responsiveness to market changes, and short product development cycles. Entrepreneurial management enables the firm to develop these specific capabilities and strategic assets in a number of ways. First, because entrepreneurial management

TABLE 5.2 Key Aspects of Entrepreneurial Management

Definition	An internal management philosophy that incorporates organizational processes and structures to promote strategic agility, flexibility, creativity, and continuous innovation
Examples	A flat organizational structure with transformational leadership throughout that empowers incumbents at all levels to proactively make informed decisions, take risks, and to be accountable for outcomes—in other words, empowers incumbents to become entrepreneurs
Key success factors	Culture that encourages and rewards curiosity, learning, and innovation; recruits and retains incumbents who tolerate ambiguity and can identify and leverage on opportunities in a cross-functional fashion and can grasp both the strategic postures and the maneuvers needed to attain its objectives
Ways to enhance capital	Promoting from within on the basis of merit; fostering organizational ownership and stewardship; rewarding risk taking, innovation, and learning, as well as an ability to work interdependently
Factors that deplete capital	Outsourcing or punishing risk-taking personnel; stagnant culture; rewarding loyalty to management rather than merit; vested interest in routines and protocols; disconnect between pay and performance

calls for systems and organizational processes where personnel curiosity, learning, and innovation are fostered and rewarded, it will be easier for the firm to develop or maintain the capability to produce repeated product innovations. Second, because firms incorporating entrepreneurial management are likely to possess a flatter, more organic structure where incumbents at all levels are empowered to make decisions, the firm will be able to respond rapidly to market changes. Third, because members of an organization employing entrepreneurial management are willing and able to think across functional domains, take calculated risks, and understand the firm's external market strategy, they are likely to be proactive and to have the skills necessary to augment the probability of short product development cycles. Thus, the organization that possesses the characteristics associated with entrepreneurial management will be empowered to develop the relevant set of strategic assets necessary to successfully implement its first-mover strategy and obtain organizational rents.

Having described the concept of entrepreneurial management and demonstrated the role it can play in the development of certain strategic assets, we now focus on ways that firm might develop and implement such management. We draw insights into the development of entrepreneurial management from the literature on organizational processes and the learning organization and from examination of the concept of *dominant logic*.

ORGANIZATIONAL PROCESSES

Organizational processes may be interpreted in more than one way. For instance, processes as a *work flow* are series of activities aimed at producing something of value. According to this perspective, business processes are viewed as a nexus of activities that combine inputs and create outputs of added value (Hammer & Champy, 1993; Johansson, 1993; Schmidt & Finnegan, 1992). Whereas work flow emphasizes the existence of clearly delineated inputs and outputs, the *coordination of work*—another process perspective—incorporates a more dynamic view of business processes. According to this view, a set of skills and routines is exploited to create capabilities that are difficult to imitate (Keen & Knapp, 1996). Indeed, sustained competitive advantage is a function of management's ability to leverage corporationwide knowledge, skills, and abilities into competencies that empower firms' constituencies to adapt quickly to changing markets and opportunities (Prahalad & Hamel, 1990; Teece, Pisano, & Shuen, 1990).

As mentioned earlier, for optimal coordination, it is crucial that managers have a broad process perspective instead of a narrow input-output perspective (e.g., work flow). Because business processes are critical to the development of organizational capabilities (and strategic assets), it is essential that managers understand the logic and dynamics behind implementing entrepreneurial management.

THE LEARNING ORGANIZATION

The learning organization (Senge, 1990), like entrepreneurial management, is an ideal prototype and represents a desired process for many firms. Incorporating radical shifts in logic and breaking from existing managerial assumptions, beliefs, and attitudes, the learning organization paradigm emphasizes people's ability to learn and implement as a source of competitive advantage. Knowledge is the foundation of organizational capabilities (Keen & Knapp, 1996), and learning organizations invest heavily in their employees. Thus, characterized by adaptive structures and cultures, learning organizations meet the forces of change with multiskilled incumbents who work relentlessly to improve their firm's strategic posture.

There are many similarities between the tenets and characteristics of the learning organization and the concept of entrepreneurial management. Like the learning organization, entrepreneurial management focuses on organizational members' autonomy as an integral part of process innovation. Both paradigms focus on how incumbents can enhance organizational effectiveness, rather than on job descriptions and work design. Entrepreneurial management, like the learning organization, calls for meeting the forces of change with workers who can think across functional domains and with an organization that is structurally, institutionally, and culturally suited for integration and flexible adaptation. Finally, both entrepreneurial management and the learning organization invest in human capital. Indeed, organizations cannot expect their members to make informed decisions and be accountable for those decisions unless they have received an adequate level of training, education, and, of course, autonomy.

In learning organizations, knowledge and integration are keys to developing organizational capabilities. However, in entrepreneurial management, nurturing a culture of curiosity and innovation complements knowledge and integration. Under entrepreneurial management, knowledge *and* curiosity are synergistically combined and semi-institutionalized, empowering incumbents to think and act as entrepreneurs do. This entails knowledge of, and curiosity about, the entire business, the environment in which it competes, and the strategies it employs to compete. The goal of entrepreneurial management is not simply to develop a smarter or more intelligent organization. Rather, it is to develop an organization in which individuals think and act with entrepreneurial autonomy. In other words, the aim of entrepreneurial management is to develop an organizational context with incumbents who proactively emulate entrepreneurs' cognitive styles and behaviors, which ultimately translates into the development of strategic assets and competitive advantage.

According to Rousseau (1997), organizational learning is similar to individual learning, particularly with respect to memory and transfer of knowledge to new situations and problems. Because shared cognitive structures are crucial for organizational learning and entrepreneurial management, smaller and more cohesive work groups may be better at harvesting their common knowledge and learning. New organizational forms (e.g., network forms, cellular forms, virtual organizations, project organizations) suggest that organizational learning and entrepreneurial management may manifest in a variety of forms. Although outsourcing can reduce internal learning and innovation (Bettis, Bradley, & Hamel, 1992), dynamic network organizations can promote learning and innovation (Miles & Snow, 1986). These dynamic network organizations are characterized by flexible memberships, identities, and job responsibilities (Miner & Robinson, 1994). By generating diverse frames of reference for problem solving, challenging old routines and systems, and harvesting organizational memory, entrepreneurial management promotes organizational learning. Job transitions (e.g., rotations, transfers, international assignments, horizontal moves, and cross-functional teams) can also promote organizational learning (via individual learning) and entrepreneurial management (via broader understanding of the business).

In sum, entrepreneurial management (i.e., flexible and adaptive work arrangements, personnel movements, reliance on expertise, and systematic information processing) makes experimentation, innovation, and collective learning paramount. As the new competitive landscape shifts firms into entrepreneurial management, more importance will be placed on enhancing organizational learning and retaining organizational knowledge.

DOMINANT LOGIC

Dominant logic is the way in which managers conceptualize the business and make resource allocation decisions (Prahalad & Bettis, 1986). The dominant logic of a firm is stored organizationally via shared schemas, cognitive maps, or mind-sets and is largely determined by the managers' and employees' experiences. An existing dominant logic may go largely unrecognized by the managers themselves (Prahalad & Bettis, 1986). Bettis and Prahalad (1995) have come to view dominant logic as an information filter. Organizational attention is focused only on information that is considered relevant with respect to the prevailing dominant logic. As a result, only relevant data and information are passed through this filter and then incorporated and institutionalized into the strategy, systems, values, expectations, and reinforced behaviors of the firm. Dominant logic is fundamental to an organization's intelligence and its ability to learn and unlearn (Bettis & Prahalad, 1995).

With respect to dominant logic, Bettis and Prahalad (1995) introduced the idea of the *unlearning curve*. That is, because previous routines and habits may inhibit the learning of new processes, some types of organizational learning require that the old logic be unlearned before new learning can occur. Although the exact relationship between the unlearning of old logic and new learning is unclear, it appears that the longer an existing logic has been in place, the more difficult it is to unlearn (Bettis & Prahalad, 1995).

The dominant logic and the unlearning curve imply obstacles for implementing changes called for by the new competitive landscape. For instance, although the learning organization and entrepreneurial management may demand radical shifts in logic and a break from existing managerial assumptions, beliefs, attitudes, and practices, these requirements are bound to be delayed by the dominant logic and the span in which unlearning takes place. Thus, for a firm to evolve into a learning organization, it must simultaneously unlearn its existing logic. It is our belief that only when effective unlearning takes place can firms develop a new dominant logic.

Institutional theory suggests that existing systems and routines become embedded in the organization and that the existing logic and processes are questioned only in times of crisis or upheaval (Oliver, 1997). Hence, firms trying to develop entrepreneurial management will face obstacles similar to those described for the learning organization. That is, to successfully employ entrepreneurial management, firms must make drastic departures from the prevailing logic associated with the hierarchical and bureaucratic processes. This suggests that entrepreneurial management may be a more viable option and relatively easier to develop in a younger firm with a less entrenched existing dominant logic or in a firm that is in a critical situation.

The concept of dominant logic may have other implications for firms attempting to develop entrepreneurial management. Recently, entrepreneurship research has found that entrepreneurs may differ from managers in large organizations in the biases, heuristics, and cognitive styles they use to view their worlds and make decisions. Busenitz and Barney (1997) found that entrepreneurs employ the biases and heuristics of *overconfidence* and *representativeness* more often than managers in large organizations. Research suggests a relationship between personality types and entrepreneurial success, with entrepreneurs being characterized as achievers, top managers, empathic salespeople, and expert idea generators (Miner, 1996). Along the same lines, Buttner and Gryskiewicz (1993) found that entrepreneurs have more "innovative" cognitive styles than do managers in large organizations, who have more "adaptive" cognitive styles. Do such findings suggest that those who combine multiple types are most likely to be successful? Although other factors are at work, including the environment, the financing available, and the strategy adopted, the implication of these findings is that it may be possible to identify individuals who possess cognitive styles and decision-making processes that are more "entrepreneurial." The ability to screen for and identify individuals who already think and act like entrepreneurs could be invaluable to firms pursuing entrepreneurial management as their dominant logic.

The previous discussions on organizational processes, learning organization, and dominant logic have clarified issues related to the development and implementation of entrepreneurial management. An examination of organizational processes and dominant logic makes it clear that leaders who strive to develop entrepreneurial management must understand the holistic nature of such ventures. Indeed, it is our view that only through the recognition that business *processes* are critical to developing certain organizational capabilities and strategic assets can managers begin to understand the logic and dynamics inherent in entrepreneurial management.

The concepts of dominant logic and unlearning emphasize the difficulty of implementing a new concept such as entrepreneurial management. They suggest that implementing entrepreneurial management may be easier and more feasible in a relatively new venture or in a venture in crisis. In this section, we also proposed that it may be possible to screen for individuals who possess more entrepreneurial cognitive and decision-making styles. This could be a critical ability for a firm pursuing entrepreneurial management and could diminish the need for a certain amount of unlearning training.

CONCLUSION

The main goal of this chapter was to present the concept of entrepreneurial management and offer some insights on its possible utility and implementation from a variety of perspectives. The introduction of the strategic assets/strategic industry factors framework (i.e., resource-based view) combined with the concept of institutional capital provides a unique perspective on the search for competitive advantage. Firms must develop not only their stocks of resource capital but also their stocks of institutional capital to maximize the rent-generating capacity of their strategic assets. A strategy of entrepreneurial management can help maximize both resource and institutional capital. More specifically, entrepreneurial management provides a possible blueprint, though admittedly in its beginning stages, for enhancing the entrepreneurial resource and institutional capital. These entrepreneurial strategic assets, characterized by flexibility and innovation, and enhanced in an entrepreneurial context, are likely to increase in importance (i.e., become strategic industry factors) in the new competitive landscape.

This chapter was inspired by the idea that management approaches could benefit from adopting more entrepreneurial strategies. We hope that by introducing the concept of entrepreneurial management we have addressed this theme and added to an emerging conceptualization of entrepreneurship as strategy.

REFERENCES

Amit, R., & Schoemaker, P. J. H. (1993). Strategic assets and organizational rent. *Strategic Management Journal, 14,* 33-46.

Barney, J. B. (1991). Asset stocks and sustained competitive advantage: A comment. *Journal of Management, 17*(1), 99-120.

Barney, J. B., & Zajac, E. J. (1994). Trustworthiness as a source of competitive advantage. *Strategic Management Journal, 15,* 5-9.

Bettis, R. A., Bradley, S. P., & Hamel, G. (1992). Outsourcing and industrial decline. *Academy of Management Executive, 6,* 7-22.

Bettis, R. A., & Hitt, M. A. (1995). The new competitive landscape, *Strategic Management Journal,* *16,* 7-19.

Bettis, R. A., & Prahalad, C. K. (1995). The dominant logic: Retrospective and extension. *Strategic Management Journal, 16,* 5-14.

Busenitz, L. W., & Barney, J. B. (1997). Differences between entrepreneurs and managers in large organizations: Biases and heuristics in strategic decision-making. *Journal of Business Venturing, 12*(1), 9-30.

Buttner, E. H., & Gryskiewicz, N. (1993). Entrepreneurs' problem-solving styles: An empirical study using the Kirton adaptation/innovation theory. *Journal of Small Business Management, 31*(1), 22-31.

Caves, R. E. (1984). Economic analysis and the quest for competitive advantage. *American Economic Review, 74,* 127-132.

Ghemawat, P. (1991a). *Commitment.* New York: Free Press.

Ghemawat, P. (1991b, May). *Resources and strategy: An IO perspective* [Mimeo]. Harvard Business School.

Hammer, M., & Champy, gentlemen. (1993). *Reengineering the corporation: A manifesto for business revolution.* New York: Harper Business.

Itami, H. (1987). *Mobilizing invisible assets.* Boston: Harvard University Press.

Johansson, H. J. (1993). *Business process engineering: Breakpoint strategies for market dominance.* New York: John Wiley.

Keen, P. G. W., & Knapp, E. (1996). *Every manager's guide to business processes.* Boston: Harvard Business School Press.

Klein, B., Crawford, R., & Alchian, A. (1978). Vertical integration, appropriable rents, and the competitive contracting process. *Journal of Law and Economics, 21,* 297-326.

Miles, R. E., & Snow, C. C. (1986). Network organizations: New concepts for new forms. *California Management Review, 28*(3), 62-73.

Miner, A. S., & Robinson, D. F. (1994). Organization and population level learning as engines for career transitions. *Journal of Organizational Behavior, 15,* 345-364.

Miner, J. B. (1996). Evidence for the existence of a set of personality types, defined by psychological tests, that predict entrepreneurial success. In P. D. Reynolds, S. Birley, J. E. Butler, W. D. Bygrave, P. Davidsson, W. B. Gartner, & P. P. McDougall (Eds.), *Frontiers of entrepreneurship research.* Wellesley, MA: Babson College, Center for Entrepreneurial Studies.

Oliver, C. (1997). Sustainable competitive advantage: Combining institutional and resource-based views. *Strategic Management Journal, 18,* 697-713.

Prahalad, C. K., & Bettis, R. A. (1986). The dominant logic: A new linkage between diversity and performance. *Strategic Management Journal, 7,* 485-501.

Prahalad, C. K., & Hamel, G. (1990). The core competence of the corporation. *Harvard Business Review, 57*(3), 79-91.

Rao, H. (1994). The social construction of reputation: Certification contests, legitimization, and the survival of organizations in the American automobile industry: 1895-1912. *Strategic Management Journal, 15,* 29-44.

Rousseau, D. M. (1997). Organizational behavior in the new organizational era. *Annual Review of Psychology, 48,* 524-546.

Schmidt, W. H., & Finnegan, J. P. (1992). *The race without a finish line: America's quest for total quality.* San Francisco: Jossey-Bass.

Schoemaker, P. J. H., & Amit, R. (1994). Investment in strategic assets: Industry and firm level perspectives. *Advances in Strategic Management, 10A,* 3-33.

Senge, P. M. (1990). *The fifth discipline.* New York: Doubleday.

Teece, D. J., Pisano, G., & Shuen, A. (1990, September). *Firm capabilities, resources, and the concept of strategy* [Mimeo]. University of California at Berkeley, Haas School of Business.

Weick, K. E. (1996). Enactment and the boundaryless career: Organizing as we work. In M. Arthur & D. M. Rousseau (Eds.), *The boundaryless career: A new employment principle for a new organizational era* (pp. 40-57). New York: Oxford University Press.

Williamson, O. (1975). *Markets and hierarchies.* New York: Free Press.

Zukin, S., & DiMaggio, P. J. (1990). Introduction. In S. Zukin & P. J. DiMaggio (Eds.), *Structures of capital: The social organization of the economy* (pp. 1-56). Cambridge, UK: Cambridge University Press.

6 | Entrepreneurial Strategies

The Critical Role of Top Management

Grant Miles
Kurt A. Heppard
Raymond E. Miles
Charles C. Snow

Any "doing things differently" in the realm of economic life should be considered an innovation and thus capable of providing a temporary advantage, and profits, to a firm.

Schumpeter (1939, p. 84)

Economies and organizations have evolved from the machine age to the information age and are now beginning to enter the knowledge age. New organizational forms have been invented during each evolutionary age to allow organizations to apply critical "know-how" to the resources that have been considered most important. This know-how has allowed firms to adapt to market demands and opportunities that have evolved from product and service standardization to customization and, most recently, to continuous innovation. In the emerging knowledge age, continuously innovative firms are likely to be characterized by self-governance, worker ownership of strategic firm assets, and entrepreneurship at all levels of the organization.

Entrepreneurship is a way of thinking about the competitive world, a way of thinking about achieving competitive advantage at a broad level, and a way of thinking about trying to find the new, the innovative, and the adaptive. Entrepreneurial strategies are certainly not the only way to gain a competitive advantage in the emerging competitive landscape, but they are going to be increasingly important for most firms. As firms pursue entrepreneurial strategies and are guided by an entrepreneurial "dominant logic" (Prahalad & Bettis, 1986), the role of top management changes dramatically. Firms move away from the concept that a CEO or a small top management team alone sets the strategic direction for the firm because it is unlikely that firms will be able to find the new, the innovative, and the adaptive solely through the efforts of top management. Instead, they will need the involvement of the entire organization. Strategy becomes, in Mintzberg's (1990) terms, much more emergent. The more traditional notion of strategy as a plan is seen only in hindsight by looking at a pattern of particular entrepreneurial actions taken by various members of the firm. Thus, managers must not only accept but also encourage the development and utilization of entrepreneurial competencies throughout the organization as one of their primary objectives.

This is a different way to think about entrepreneurial strategies, and it implies a new role for top managers. This chapter focuses on critical aspects of this new role. Top managers must first develop a strategic vision for the firm. They must also select and implement an organizational form that is most likely to support this strategic vision. We discuss an emerging organizational form, the cellular form, as one that is likely to be particularly important in entrepreneurial strategies. Top executives must also adopt a new managerial philosophy, the human investment philosophy, to reap the greatest gains from entrepreneurial strategies. Finally, and perhaps most importantly, managers must build organizations where members at all levels of the organization have the opportunity to develop and use their entrepreneurial competencies.

STRATEGIC VISION

To set the stage for entrepreneurial strategies, top management must develop and institute a strategic vision for the firm that is conducive to entrepreneurial action. This vision will typically cover both content (e.g., the scope of the firm's efforts) and the processes necessary to achieve this (e.g., the focus on entrepreneurial actions and the broad guidelines for promoting such actions). This vision, however, must be broad rather than specific, because too much structure may serve to inhibit the very actions that the vision is trying to promote.

In terms of the scope of work, it is necessary for top management to set at least broad parameters for the nature of innovation that will be encouraged. An important aspect of these guidelines is a determination of whether the firm will concentrate primarily on products or processes. Although a firm can be entrepreneurial or innovative in either of those areas, most firms do not typically do well at both. Therefore, the direction from the top addresses whether the firm will focus primarily on the product or service, "the outcome," or whether the firm will focus more on the process, "the how" of producing the outcome.

The second area covered by the vision is an effort to promote entrepreneurial actions throughout the firm. The traditional organization does not typically reward or even encourage entrepreneurial action, except perhaps among a small handful of managers at the upper levels of the organization. Thus, lower-level employees are not likely to pursue such actions on their own. Management must therefore find ways to establish that entrepreneurial activity will not only be tolerated but in fact be encouraged for all employees. Although several things might be done in this regard, an underlying theme must be the "legitimization of cooperation" (Miles & Miles, 1998) because cooperation both within the organization and across organizations is likely to be necessary for successful entrepreneurship.

Entrepreneurial activity is by its nature a creative process that must be relatively unconstrained if it is to operate effectively. At the same time, however, people have to be moving in the same basic direction if the firm is to survive and prosper over time. The strategic vision, then, seeks to balance these needs, providing general guidance, direction, and encouragement, yet also providing the latitude necessary to promote entrepreneurial activity.

SELECTION OF ORGANIZATIONAL FORM

A second critical action taken by top management is the selection or setting of the organizational form. Like the strategic vision, the form must provide both structure and freedom for organizational actions. The selection of organizational form is a strategic choice that puts a system or set of routines in place that will allow strategy and entrepreneurship to emerge anywhere in the organization.

The notion of organizational form is really the representational logic of the firm. It describes a pattern of strategy, structure, and processes that both organizes and directs the firm. Forms are a useful metaphor because they help explain the overarching logic of the operating, investment, and adaptation routines that are the means by which organizations add value (Miles, Miles, & Snow, 1998). The form both promotes the efficiency and effectiveness of the routines and serves as a storehouse for the know-how that is contained within the routines.

To be successful, however, the routines being emphasized and pursued have to fit the logic of the form. This is important to recognize when considering the impact of a form on entrepreneurial activities. Although traditional forms such as the functional or multidivisional structures all have particular strengths, their underlying logic is geared toward a hierarchical process that directs work activities. Because entrepreneurship is typically a horizontal process that works better without much interference from management, entrepreneurial activities may be in conflict with traditional ways of organizing. Although some of the problems associated with this may be overcome through the use of various lateral coordination mechanisms (Galbraith, 1994), the inherent conflict is likely to limit the effectiveness of the firm over time.

To successfully pursue entrepreneurial activities, then, managers need to select a form that works in concert with such activities. That is, they need to create an infrastructure that supports lateral communication and coordination efforts while allowing the workers the freedom necessary to pursue entrepreneurial ideas without the direct intervention of upper management. As well, the form must allow for linkages and interaction between the organization and the external environment.

Vincenzo Perrone (personal communication, 1998), a professor at Bocconi University in Milan, has broadly described this form as requiring a "double net." By this he means that the organization exists in the complex external characteristics of an external network of firms but at the same time maintains a comparable level of internal complexity—a sort of requisite variety inside the firm. The internal firm must be as complex and as adaptive as the network itself.

Networks are increasingly being turned to as a means of responding to a rapidly changing and increasingly competitive environment. The notion is that by creating a loosely coupled system of otherwise independent firms, the broader system can more quickly respond to demands for change. In practice, however, the network can only respond as fast as the slowest firm within the chain. Firms that behave well in networks seem to have an ability to "rotate." That is, they make extensive use of teams and other lateral mechanisms both within the firm and between the firm and its partners so that they are able to shift resources to meet the demands of the environment and entrepreneurial opportunities of the marketplace.

THE CELLULAR FORM

In the most advanced organizational forms, not only are there mechanisms for rotating or shifting firm resources for quicker and more efficient utilization, but there are also mechanisms that allow the firm to simultaneously grow new resources. In trying to describe these firms, Miles, Snow, Mathews, Miles, and Coleman (1997) borrowed the term *cellular,* which several others had used earlier in a somewhat related fashion. The cellular concept helps describe a form in which each piece shares characteristics with all the other pieces of the whole. That is true of cellular organisms—each cell has the essential properties of the larger organism. When cells are combined, however, there is something far richer than the individual cell.

The cellular notion captures the idea of continuous evolution and continuous growth, a biological phenomenon. This is what appears to be happening in the most advanced entrepreneurial firms and pieces of firms. Units are self-governing, self-coordinating, and self-initiating. They are responsible for their own entrepreneurship and for regenerating their own resources and expanding their own resources. This is what a living organism is called on to do. We think we are seeing an evolution of a form, including an underlying logic of governance skills, technical skills, and adaptation skills, that allows for almost complete utilization of the know-how currently within the firm and, simultaneously, the generation of new know-how in such a way that the firm can conceivably be continuously innovative. The organization can always do new things because it is able to use all that it knew before as well as all the know-how that it is generating. It knows how to continue to generate that know-how.

It seems that this cellular form is emerging widely in knowledge industries, as well as in firms involved in the design segments of networks in many other industries. In these firms, every cell—that is, every team or unit—is able to make use of all of the know-how available in every other cell. Moreover, the protocols in these firms are designed to make every activity a shared learning experience. Older organizational forms have difficulty applying know-how to the generation and use of new knowledge. However, this ability is the critical competence in settings where knowledge is the key resource employed. In sum, when you examine the cellular metaphor, when you use it to understand what is occurring in organizations, the possibility of almost continuous, efficient innovation and entrepreneurship is not such a bizarre notion.

An example of a "complete" cellular organization pursuing an entrepreneurial strategy is Technical and Computer Graphics (TCG). TCG is an information technology company that develops a wide range of electronic products and services, including hand-held data terminals for loggers, computer graphics systems, and electronic interchange systems. Within the corporate body of TCG, there are 13 individual firms that share a common vision and some features but maintain the ability to function independently of their other sister firms. Each of the various firms has developed its own unique technical and business competencies. As part of its operating logic, however, TCG has developed a process of "triangulation" that allows the firm to continuously evolve and be entrepreneurial. At TCG, triangulation is really a partnership that involves three central pieces connected through a lead firm within TCG. These partners include a principal customer, an external firm participating as a joint venture partner (typically for manufacturing), and one or more TCG firms that provide additional skills and expertise to the project.

TCG's strategy is entrepreneurial in the sense that each of its internal firms is expected to continuously search for new product and service opportunities. When an internal firm manager believes that a new venture shows technological promise and potential profitability, the process of triangulation begins. The first step is finding an external customer for the proposed product or service. The intent is to presell the customer so that the customer will provide at least some of the up-front funding for the project. Early identification of a customer also may allow for customization of the proposed offering that might make it more attractive. With a customer identified, an external joint venture partner is then sought. Like the customer, this partner is expected to provide some initial funding, similar to venture capital, as well as collaboration and knowledge in the development of the product. Finally, there is a search for partners within TCG. Rather than being dictated by top management, however, each firm with a project must sell other internal firms on participating in the project and providing necessary skills and abilities. In return, the internal partners may get a piece of the profits, access to the customer, and/or an opportunity for learning and development.

This entrepreneurial approach allows TCG to continuously learn how to produce new, state-of-the-art products that are tailor made to a principal customer's specifications. At the same time, the internal triangulation with other cells within TCG helps to spread knowledge and propagate critical business development, partnering, and project management competencies. The three important entrepreneurial characteristics of the cellular organization at TCG are the following:

1. The acceptance of individual responsibility and viability, which are the cornerstones of the overall cellular concept of "firms within a firm"
2. The commitment to self-organization and self-governance, which gives individual firms within the company the flexibility and strategic latitude to pursue new technological challenges, beneficial partnering relationships, and evolving customer and market demands
3. The responsibility to be individually profitable as well as to share profitability with other TCG firms through internal partnerships

These three characteristics are the building blocks of the cellular organizational form at TCG and vital components of emerging entrepreneurial strategies in the evolving knowledge age economy.

SHIFTING TOWARD A NEW ORGANIZATIONAL FORM

In theory, management is free to select the organizational form of the company. In practice, however, a number of constraints are likely to be faced. The reality is that older, more established firms typically are unable simply to change form, as a newer, smaller firm can, or to start with an entrepreneurial form, as a start-up firm might be able to do. It is important to realize, though, that such constraints can at times be more perceptual than real. For example, at Oticon, a large, established Danish hearing aid manufacturer, the CEO made a decision to change the entire form in a very short period of time (Labarre, 1996). The transition has not always been easy, and some of the details of how the form should now work have had to emerge over time. Still, it all started with a CEO who made a conscious, deliberate, fundamental decision to move the firm from a functional hierarchy to a form that removed barriers in the organization and promoted entrepreneurial actions.

Can this radical a change be made in very large organizations such as an IBM or General Motors? Probably not, but there are still things that such companies can do and are doing to affect organizational form. It is important to recognize that forms are a package of not only structure but also strategies and processes and that the groundwork for the change may be laid by changing these aspects of the package. Rather than walking in one day and announcing, "Here is a new organizational form, and it's going to operate on the basis of new protocols rather than established rules and regulations," one can take steps that begin to adjust cultures and thinking so that the organization is ready for a shift when the time comes. An important part of this process is shifting the way that managers view both their own role and the role of workers, a point addressed in the next section.

THE HUMAN INVESTMENT
PHILOSOPHY FOR MANAGERS

As organizational forms have evolved over time, there have been complementary shifts in the underlying philosophies that effective managers have held about workers and what they can contribute. In seeking both to understand and to describe how managers actually think about the process of managing an organization, three aspects of that process can be identified. These include the managers' assumptions about people, the resulting policies that are pursued, and the expectations about what will happen under these conditions (Miles, 1965).

In the earliest days of large-scale organization, these philosophies centered on the notion of strict managerial control. As reflected in the work of Frederick Taylor, this view held that workers could not be trusted and were interested only in earning a paycheck. As a result, policies of heavy supervision and direction were the norm. The expectation was that given these conditions, management could expect a decent day's work from most employees.

A second approach, human relations theory, first appeared in the 1910s and 1920s and then flowered in the 1950s. It was built on a belief that people had some elements of competency. The manager's primary task was to deal with their employees' human needs of belonging and feeling important. It was believed that managers should adopt a leadership style that involved people in discussions and that managers should seek the opinions of employees, not so much to actually use their opinions as to make people feel a part of the organization. It was thought that this would make workers more satisfied in their jobs and therefore possibly more productive.

Although the human relations movement started the process of employee involvement, it did not take it all that far. In the 1960s, however, Miles (1965) contrasted the human relations model with what he saw as an emerging managerial view. Managers holding this new philosophy, called human resources, truly believed that employees were capable of doing much more than they were typically asked for and that the job of management was to tap the underutilized capabilities of the members of their organizations. In the organizations of the 1960s and 1970s, there were many underutilized capabilities, and managers who aggressively set out to unleash those capabilities usually made enormous contributions to the organization. In doing so, policies for truly involving workers were developed through mechanisms such as self-directed teams and employee empowerment. The resulting expectation was that workers would be even more productive and valuable to the organization. Managers holding this view believed that as a by-product, the new approach would be satisfying to workers in the same way that it was satisfying to them.

The notions underlying the human resources model were not necessarily new. In many ways, they can be traced back to the work of Edith Penrose (1959) and her work on the theory of the growth of the firm. To be more than marginally accepted, however, these philosophies had to be combined with development of organizational forms that could accommodate them. In a like manner, the evolution into the current advanced organizational forms, such as cellular, seems to be unleashing a further advancement in managerial philosophies. The human investment philosophy takes the next evolutionary step in the discussion of the utilization of the capabilities of employees. Like the human resources view, it is characterized by a belief in the untapped capabilities of employees. But it is also characterized by a belief that, through training and education, employees are capable of learning and developing well beyond their current capabilities. The expectation is that this investment in training will be returned to the organization in the form of continual organizational learning.

To achieve this learning, however, managers must be ready to redefine their relationship with workers. Traditional hierarchies put managers at the top, when, in fact, the pyramid should really be inverted. Given that it is the people at the bottom of the pyramid who really do the work, management's focus should be on supporting them. The human investment philosophy states that management's job is not to control, monitor, and supervise. Instead, management's job is to develop the workers and provide opportunities for them to use their capabilities, including entrepreneurial competencies.

The human investment notion differs from the human resources model only in the sense that managers in an increasingly complex world must go a step further in their beliefs. They must be prepared to risk investing in the growth of capabilities at the level of the individual worker and the work team. This investment is risky because, in the highly mobile, downsized organizations of today and tomorrow, the investments that managers make in their workforce may not always be easily measured in terms of direct impact on the organization and its performance. That is, the results of investing in people cannot be accounted for as easily as the results of investing in more traditional tangible assets such as property and equipment (Miles, Miles, Perrone, & Edvennson, 1998).

In addition, managers have to be prepared for the fact that they may be investing in training for people who are likely to leave the organization. By their nature, entrepreneurial strategies encourage workers to find the greatest opportunity to profitably use their skills, whether that is in their current position or in another position at another firm. A reality in today's downsized world is that there is not always room for everyone to be promoted or given the opportunities he or she deserves. Managers facing these conditions must hope that other firms are training workers with the same entrepreneurial drive and competencies and must be willing to bring in new employees who have been trained in other organizations.

At the same time, however, management can control this loss of workers by continually seeking to increase the opportunities for entrepreneurial action within the firm. The human investment philosophy requires not only a commitment to continuous investment in the growth of human resources but also a commitment to fully utilizing human resources, including entrepreneurial competencies. Although earlier forms and philosophies have gone a long way in pushing down decision making and increasing the freedom of action for many workers, cellular forms, human investment philosophies, and the search for entrepreneurial strategies require taking this involvement to the extreme. In these organizations, every member must have not only adaptation, governance, and entrepreneurial competencies but also the opportunity to use them.

RECRUITMENT AND TRAINING

Full implementation of the human investment philosophy requires that managers treat all employees as if they have the capability to be entrepreneurial. However, experience suggests that this is not likely to be the case. There are in fact likely to be some workers who simply do not have the requisite variety of skills for entrepreneurial activity. In addition, there are probably a fair number of people who, despite having the ability to take on more challenging assignments, are simply more comfortable with traditional management approaches. They want to know what their job is, and they don't want a great deal of ambiguity in their daily work lives. They prefer to have an hourly rate, earn overtime, go home, and forget about the job. They like to have the ability to say no and to avoid responsibility. So not only do the managers need to have a human investment philosophy, but they also need to find workers who believe in the human investment approach.

As a general rule, advanced organizational forms, human investment philosophies, and entrepreneurial strategies are more likely to be successful in industries that employ large numbers of professionals. Though one is hesitant to generalize too far, professionals have typically gravitated toward their positions because they had a bent toward self-direction and preferred situations where there were not a great number of constraints imposed by management. There are, however, blue-collar workers who would thrive under a human investment philosophy and an entrepreneurial strategy, and there are some professionals who could not handle it.

Thus, managers need to consider both the nature of their recruiting process and the situations in which the employees will be working.

These notions are incredibly challenging for organizations and for managers who were trained with a different set of assumptions about workers and their role in the firm. Given the emphasis on downsizing and outsourcing in recent years, it has been relatively easy for managers to make almost no human resource investments. They have been able to simply reach out and grab resources from someone else's organization. Only very far-sighted managers have recognized the need to renew the competencies in their own organization and to develop entrepreneurial ones. Such managers have also recognized that in the newer organizational forms there are greater requirements for adaptation and entrepreneurship. There is a need to train deeper in the organization. Peter Drucker (1954) once had the notion that an ideal organization behaved in such a way that every person thought like a manager: That is, everyone had managerial vision. This is the type of organizational reality that must evolve in advanced organizational forms and entrepreneurial strategies. Everyone in the organization must have entrepreneurial vision *and* managerial competence. That is a view of the ultimate organizational form that is currently imaginable. Everyone is an entrepreneur; everyone is a coordinator; everyone is a facilitator; everyone is a professional. You only get there with very heavy investment and reinvestment in human resources.

ENTREPRENEURIAL COMPETENCIES

Through a package that includes promoting an entrepreneurial vision, establishing an appropriate advanced organizational form, and incorporating a human investment philosophy at all levels of the organization, management should quickly begin to see the emergence of entrepreneurial competencies appropriate for implementing entrepreneurial strategies. These competencies include the ability to recognize new market opportunities and to identify and assemble the resources necessary to meet them. Probably the most important notion in developing entrepreneurial competencies, however, is that workers at all levels of the organization must have the opportunity and freedom to utilize them.

Many managers are not ready to give up this much control. They are fearful of the risks inherent in entrepreneurial actions and therefore want employees to "run ideas by management" before the ideas are implemented. Such concerns and fears are certainly understandable. If they cannot be overcome, however, the company should give serious consideration to foregoing the notion of entrepreneurial strategies.

Entrepreneurial ideas, by their nature, are time bound and subject to expiration. Although "running ideas by management" may seem prudent, it is likely to present a bottleneck that works against the success of the approaches. More importantly, it is likely to stifle the entrepreneurial spirit of the employees. Entrepreneurial competencies can be developed and refined only through use over time. No opportunity, no competencies. No opportunity, no motivation.

What is more, this freedom of opportunity must be pushed well down into the organization. A priori, it is seldom clear where entrepreneurial opportunities will arise. Thus, limiting the level at which entrepreneurial action can take place is likely to mean significant missed opportunities. Again, we recognize that the notion of allowing entrepreneurial action at lower levels may be frightening for managers trained in traditional approaches. If the package of ideas described above is accepted, however, it will become an expected result rather than a frightful thought.

The reality is that most workers want to contribute, and many of them have good ideas that may help the company. The problem is unleashing it. There is a consulting firm in Sweden that has done very well coming into companies that want to be more entrepreneurial. With the blessing of management, they have essentially presented an offer to the employees that says, "The company is interested in new ideas and new ways of doing things, but they don't have money to pay up front in order to support these new ideas until they have been developed more fully. This consulting group is here to help you develop ideas." The group has had some very good success in finding employees eager to develop their new ideas even in companies that didn't feel they had any real entrepreneurial talents in the organization. Of course, not all ideas work, but finding that many employees want to be creative and entrepreneurial and make a difference for the company is revealing. The success suggests that there is a lot more entrepreneurial talent inside organizations than many CEOs currently realize. Finding such talent, of course, is not the same as finding ways to profitably unleash it. Putting together a vision, a form, and a philosophy that support entrepreneurial strategies, however, is a big step toward getting there.

REFERENCES

Drucker, P. F. (1954). *The practice of management.* New York: Harper & Brothers.

Galbraith, J. R. (1994). *Competing with flexible lateral organizations.* Reading, MA: Addison-Wesley.

Labarre, P. (1996, June/July). This organization is dis-organization. *Fast Company,* pp. 5-9.

Miles, G., Miles, R. E., Perrone, V., & Edvennson, L. (1998). Some conceptual and research barriers to the utilization of knowledge. *California Management Review, 40,* 281-288.

Miles, R. E. (1965). Human relations or human resources. *Harvard Business Review, 43,* 148-163.

Miles, R. E., & Miles, G. (1998). Leadership and collaboration. In J. Conger, G. Spreitzer, & E. Lawler (Eds.), *The leader's change handbook* (pp. 321-343). San Francisco: Jossey-Bass.

Miles, R. E., Miles, G., & Snow, C. (1998). Good for practice: An integrated theory of the value of alternative organizational forms. In G. Hamel, C. K. Prahalad, H. Thomas, & D. O'Neil (Eds.), *Strategic flexibility: Managing in a turbulent environment* (pp. 93-114). New York: John Wiley.

Miles, R. E., Snow, C., Mathews, J., Miles, G., & Coleman, H., Jr. (1997). Organizing in the knowledge age: Anticipating the cellular form. *Academy of Management Executive, 11*(4), 7-20.

Penrose, E. (1959). *The theory of the growth of the firm.* Oxford, UK: Basil Blackwell.

Mintzberg, H. (1990). Strategy formation: Schools of thought. In J. W. Fredrickson, *Perspectives on strategic management,* pp. 105-236. New York: Harper and Row.

Prahalad, C., & Bettis, R. (1986). The dominant logic: A new link between diversity and performance. *Strategic Management Journal, 7,* 485-501.

Schumpeter, J. A. (1939). *Business cycles* (Vol. 1). New York: McGraw-Hill.

7 | The Evolution of the Field of Entrepreneurship

Arnold C. Cooper
Gideon D. Markman
Gayle Niss

This chapter is concerned with the evolution of entrepreneurship as an academic field of study. We shall review briefly the history of the development of the field and its current position. Then we shall consider future prospects, noting factors both outside and inside universities that seem likely to bear on the field. Entrepreneurship will be considered both as it relates to new venture creation and as it relates to making existing organizations more flexible and innovative. We shall note how the study of entrepreneurship initially was concerned with small business management and new venture creation but evolved, over time, to include a larger population of firms, including established organizations seeking to revitalize themselves.

The evolution of an academic field of study may appear, on first consideration, to be of interest only to academics. However, we suggest that the development of the field has implications not only for entrepreneurs but also for public policy makers, managers, and the general public. The development of a knowledge base about the field should help both existing entrepreneurs and those who aspire to create their own businesses, as well as their advisors. For public policy and strategy makers concerned with economic development, entrepreneurship offers promise as a source of job creation and innovation. For managers, entrepreneurial strategies suggest ways to revitalize existing organizations and make them more innovative. As entrepreneurship contributes to a more vital and innovative economy, the public can benefit from new jobs, services, and products that become available.

ENTREPRENEURSHIP:
THE PAST

As an academic field of study, entrepreneurship and entrepreneurship strategy are quite young. Myles Mace offered the first course in entrepreneurship, "Management of New Enterprises," at the Harvard Business School in 1947. Peter Drucker started a course in entrepreneurship and innovation at New York University in 1953. Most of the early courses dealt primarily with new venture creation and small business management, and it was a number of years before many business schools began to focus on entrepreneurial strategies within established organizations. The first conference on small business management was held at St. Gallen University in Switzerland in 1948. This biennial conference held its 50th anniversary conference in the fall of 1998. Sponsored by the Center for Venture Management, the first academic conference on entrepreneurship research in the United States was held at Purdue University in 1970. At the Academy of Management meetings in 1974, Karl Vesper held an organizational meeting for those interested in entrepreneurship. It led to an Entrepreneurship Interest Group, initially part of the Division of Business Policy and Planning. This group did not achieve full status as an independent division of the Academy of Management until 1987.

The first international conference on entrepreneurship research was held in Toronto in 1973. At that time, there was an effort to organize a new professional organization, the Society for Entrepreneurship Research and Application (SERA). This society, however, never progressed beyond its original mailing list of 42 members. In 1975, the International Symposium of Entrepreneurship and Enterprise Development (ISEED) took place in Cincinnati. This ambitious undertaking attracted participants from all over the world. Babson College played a major role in the early development of the field. It established the Academy of Distinguished

Entrepreneurs in 1978 to recognize "world-class" entrepreneurs. This became a prototype of other programs to recognize entrepreneurs, their accomplishments, and achievements, including the Ernst & Young Entrepreneur of the Year Awards, the National Federation of Independent Business (NFIB) Best in America contest, and others. The Babson Research Conference started in 1981 as a working conference in which all participants had to have some current and cutting-edge research to report on. Although the organizers were not sure whether there would be enough new research to justify annual conferences, it continues to grow and thrive. Another important initiative was the Small Business Institute (SBI) Program, which started in 1972 at Texas Tech University and provided support to universities that gave courses on consulting to small businesses. This program developed rapidly, with 396 universities participating by 1976.

For many years, there were few publishing outlets for work on entrepreneurship. In 1963, the *Journal of Small Business Management* was launched under the auspices of the National Council for Small Business. In 1975, the *American Journal of Small Business* was started. Its name was later changed to *Entrepreneurship Theory and Practice* under the leadership of Ray Bagby in 1988. In 1985, Ian MacMillan started the *Journal of Business Venturing* with the sponsorship of New York University and the Wharton School. *Explorations in Entrepreneurial History* (subsequently entitled *Explorations in Economic History*) was published at Harvard and then at the University of Wisconsin. In 1989, Zoltan Acs and David Audretsch launched the *Journal of Small Business Economics*. Other recent journals include *Small Business Strategy* (1990), *Family Business Review* (1988), and *Journal of Developmental Entrepreneurship* (1996).

In a review of these developments, one thing stands out. Most of the conferences and journals that are devoted to entrepreneurship have been started in the last 20 years. Entrepreneurship as a distinct academic field of study is indeed young.

Although there has been an enormous increase in the number of courses in the field, the number of people able to devote their full energies to teaching and research in entrepreneurship is still quite limited. Non-tenure-track faculty or adjuncts, often on a part-time basis, teach many of the courses. Although these are often fine teachers, their other commitments are such that they are usually not involved in developing the intellectual capital of the field. Even where tenure-track faculties are involved, their primary teaching and writing is often in other areas (such as general strat-egy), and entrepreneurship per se takes a secondary role. Furthermore, many of these faculties are most concerned with application and are less inclined toward research and theory development.

ENTREPRENEURSHIP: THE PRESENT

The current state of entrepreneurship reflects tremendous growth along almost all dimensions. The number of educational institutions with entrepreneurship courses has increased from fewer than 10 in 1967 (Vesper, 1993) to 400 in 4-year colleges and 600 in community colleges (Ballon, 1998). (These surveys primarily reflect courses in new venture creation and small business management rather than courses in entrepre-neurial strategy or in making existing organizations more entrepreneurial.) Many schools now offer majors in entrepreneurship, and many of these courses and programs are very popular. *Success Magazine* now requires schools to offer a minimum of three graduate-level courses in entrepre-neurship or entrepreneurial strategy even to be considered in its annual ratings of entrepreneurship programs. The number of scientific journals has grown to 27, with at least 10 outside the United States. In fact, a recent count indicated that more than 700 papers are presented at conferences annually (Welsch & Klandt, 1997). Chaired professorships have been added at many schools, and Katz (1997) reported that in 1997 there were at least 171 chaired professorships. More than 100 universities have estab-lished entrepreneurship centers that serve as focal points for research, business outreach, student enrichment, and fund-raising programs.

Public interest in entrepreneurship is reflected in the increase in the number of references in the general press. In 1997, ABI/Inform and Lexis-Nexis reported over 10,000 journal and newspaper listings of entrepreneurship-related literature. This compares with less than 2,000 twelve years earlier. The extent to which entrepreneurship has captured the public imagination is illustrated in a *USA Today* survey that asked young people, "If you could devote 1 year to any occupation, what would you choose?" Women and men both chose "being an entrepreneur" as their first choice, 47% and 38% respectively, which was even more than being a "professional athlete." Similarly, a Gallup poll reported that over

90% of Americans would approve if their children started a small business (Dennis, 1997a). This widespread interest in entrepreneurship is occurring in many countries outside the United States as well.

We argue that the widespread interest in new venture creation and in entrepreneurial strategy reflects the new economy. Not only are new ventures being created at unprecedented rates, but existing organizations are being transformed by leveraging entrepreneurial strategies. Traditionally, authority flowed from the top down, and managers had limited scope for autonomous action. Organizational power was derived from control over tangible resources, number of reporting subordinates, and organizational position. Similarly, incumbents were valued for their loyalty and ability to follow routines and instructions. In the new competitive era of the knowledge economy, the ability to network, self-manage, and cope with uncertainties, along with speed and agility, is valued. This means that to improve employment prospects, incumbents should strive to develop social and human capital in addition to technical skills (Baron & Markman, in press).

The changing demographics of many organizations is consistent with *Fortune Magazine's* estimate that the average young person entering the job market will have 10 different jobs with five different organizations before retirement. The disappearance of entire categories of jobs and the parallel increase in the value of personal employability (rather than job security) parallel the decline of well-known organizations and even industries. Hitt and Ireland (1987), who compared Peters and Waterman's (1984) "excellent firms" with a sample of Fortune 1,000 firms, showed that only three of the "excellent firms" performed better than the *average* of the Fortune 1,000 sample. Moreover, several of the Fortune 1,000 firms outperformed all existing "excellent firms," not to mention that many of the "excellent" companies in Peters and Waterman's book no longer exist. It appears that the shifting lines of authority, the blurring boundaries of incumbents' control, and the eroding loyalty and sense of affiliation of employees are resulting in a business environment that is very different from what it was not only 25 to 30 years ago, but even 5 years ago.

In the late 1960s, when entrepreneurship as an academic field was just starting and little attention was devoted to entrepreneurial strategies, many assumed that large corporations were likely to dominate the economy and that smaller firms would play only a marginal role. Today we know that this is not the case. For instance, in 1969, only 274,000 new corporations were started; in 1995, the annual number had reached 770,000. Furthermore, when all organizational forms and part-time and home-based businesses are counted, the total number of start-ups is on the order of 4.5 million per year (Dennis, 1997b). In 1972, the Fortune 500 companies accounted for 19.9% of the nonfarm employment, but since then, employment accounted for by these firms has declined steadily and in 1991 was down to 10.9%. In the United States, Fortune 1,000 firms lost 3.5 million jobs during the decade of the 1980s. During that same period, firms with less than 500 employees added 10 million new jobs. We will argue that the wide recognition that new and innovative firms are a vital part of our economy (Venkataraman, in press) has led to two interrelated trends. First, the significance of entrepreneurship as an academic field is continuing to grow. Second, entrepreneurial strategy has begun to be viewed as a potential source of firms' competitive advantage, a way in which established firms can develop capabilities that are central to their continuing success.

ENTREPRENEURSHIP:
THE FUTURE

The academic field of entrepreneurship has been flourishing, but will it continue to thrive in the future? Or will this later be viewed as a field that was popular for a time and then was replaced by other "hot" topics? Much will depend on whether the environmental trends that have led to increased entrepreneurial activities and strategies will continue. If rates of new venture formation persist and if there continues to be great interest in developing entrepreneurial capabilities in existing organizations, then the academic fields of entrepreneurial strategy and new venture creation should continue to attract students, scholars, and financial support. Here we consider some of the drivers of entrepreneurship and entrepreneurial strategy, factors that seem likely to bear on the future development of the field.

KNOWLEDGE AND TECHNOLOGY-BASED ECONOMY

The turbulence of the new competitive landscape (see Chapter 2) creates market disequilibrium and remarkable growth opportunities (Dean,

Meyer, & DeCastro, 1993). More specifically, uncertainty and disequilibrium expose markets to new ideas and thus create favorable milieus for new venture creation or for organizations able to develop entrepreneurial strategies. Although high rates of change create opportunities for both new and mature firms, it is young firms that do not have a stake in the status quo. According to Hitt and Bartkus (1997), the competitive landscape has altered such that disequilibrium and uncertainty offset economies of size and scale advantages. For instance, although the small-firm segment of the economy spends only a fraction of what large firms spend on R&D, proportionally small firms tend to be more R&D efficient (Cooper, 1964). In terms of tangible outcomes, small firms account for more than half of all major product innovations in the United States (Acs, 1996). Moreover, many industries characterized by high rates of innovation also have high rates of new venture creation. Thus, as changing technologies transform our economy, entrepreneurial ventures are expected to play a major role (Zahra, 1996). These changes also lead to the recognition that entrepreneurial strategies can be a source of sustainable competitive advantage in a rapidly changing world.

INCREASING IMPORTANCE OF SERVICES

A characteristic of the new economy is the continued growth of the service sector. In considering jobs generated by sector from 1991 to 1996, the annual growth in jobs in services was 3.4%, far higher than for other sectors. This growth was concentrated in small service firms. Service firms with more than 100 employees added jobs at a rate of only 0.8% per year. Those with fewer than 100 employees grew at 7.2% per year (*Corporate Almanac,* 1996; *Who's Creating Jobs?* 1996). Of the 1997 Inc. 500 firms ("Inc. 500," 1997) (all high-growth firms), 59% were in the service sector. Indeed, such rapidly growing entrepreneurial firms provide the backbone for job creation and thus economic growth. Because these firms—as compared to nonentrepreneurial firms—produce higher rates of return on investment, use more debt financing, and earn superior returns on invested equity capital, their capital use is highly effective. Thus, the growth of services and the capital efficiency of the entrepreneurial firms within this sector are likely to contribute to the continued development of new ventures.

DOWNSIZING, REENGINEERING,
AND NEW EMPLOYMENT FORMS

The downsizing of many corporations during the 1980s and 1990s yielded stunning layoff statistics, though occasionally disappointing productivity improvement. Millions of workers were laid off as companies attempted to become leaner and more responsive to global competition (Byrne, 1994; Maney, 1994; Schmit, 1994). Middle managers and first-line employees have been particularly hard hit by so-called *delayering*. Some companies went from 13 layers of management in 1985 to 5 layers in 1992 (Sookdeo, 1992). And just when the downsizing and delayering era seemed to be nearing its end, emphasis on *reengineering* emerged. Involving a radical redesign of the entire organization, reengineering aimed at dramatically improving performance via efficiency and quality (Champy, 1995). As corporations have reexamined their routines and strategies and considered which competencies should be retained and which should be farmed out to others, employment in the Fortune 500 companies has been declining.

The revolution of downsizing, delayering, restructuring, and reengineering is nothing less than a direct assault on the once-unquestioned notion of corporate hierarchy and incumbents' entitlement mentality. These changes reflect the shift from traditional to entrepreneurial strategies and management. That is, old management paradigms fostered learning one skill, striving to maintain the status quo and a top-down hierarchy, and viewing capital mostly as equipment. Management based on entrepreneurial strategies, on the other hand, focuses on risk-taking, job creation, and lifelong learning, where speed, change, and intellectual capitals are essential. Table 7.1 summarizes some of the characteristics of traditional management and entrepreneurial strategies.

Whether they intend to start new ventures or to be contributing employees in established organizations, incumbents must continually develop new knowledge, skills, and abilities. Managers are required both to unlearn some of their managerial paradigms and established routines and to quickly develop new capabilities, including novel leadership styles and awareness of ways to make their organizations more entrepreneurial. In organizations that develop entrepreneurial strategies, repetitive tasks are becoming nonrepetitive, tenure-track positions and job descriptions are vanishing, and role-based jobs are forming around knowledge and

TABLE 7.1   Characteristics of traditional management and entrepreneurship

Traditional Management	Entrepreneurial Strategies
Security and job preservation	Risk taking and job creation
Learning one skill	Lifelong learning
Stability, tradition, consistency, robustness	Speed, change, adaptability, agility
Top-down command, hierarchical structure	360-degree integration, flat structure
Capital is equipment	Capital is people's know-how
Regulation	Deregulation
Segregation and compartmentalization	Integration and synergy
Transaction and control	Transformation and empowerment
Status is ascribed	Status is achieved
Scarcity mentality, zero-sum game	Abundance mentality, win-win paradigm

personal initiatives (Rousseau, 1997). New employment models (i.e., telecommuting, independent contractors, and temporary workers) that imply diminished managerial authority also put pressure on managers to change their style and techniques. Limited managerial authority and the concurrent rise in knowledge-based industries challenge structures and command lines typically associated with traditional management styles. With fewer managerial controls over workers, greater value is placed on improvisation, curiosity, learning, and ultimately innovation (Weick, 1996), all of which are obvious trademarks of entrepreneurship. It therefore appears that entrepreneurial strategy will continue to thrive and have an impact in many organizational settings.

NEW ORGANIZATIONAL
FORMS AND ALLIANCES

Because of mounting competition and, in some cases, stagnant productivity, many organizations are searching for ways to build competitive advantage. These pressures produce new organizational forms that attempt to combine strategy, structure, and management processes (Miles & Snow, 1986). New organizational forms (e.g., dynamic networks and cellular organizations, which may include the development of internal and external brokering, vertical disaggregation, disclosed information systems, and market substitutes for administrative mechanisms) prompt more reliance on self-managed work units and lead to permeable organizational boundaries. Virtual corporations increasingly outsource not only support functions but also basic activities such as production and sales. Such strategies also make it possible for new firms to get established without large investments while relying upon others to make, sell, and finance their products. The concept of the virtual corporation, in which firms increasingly outsource not only peripheral functions but also core activities, creates opportunities for entrepreneurs.

The intense interest in seeking competitive advantage via new structures has led to the forging of interfirm alliances and permeability of company boundaries (D'Aveni, 1994). Alliances, including cooperative agreements among two or more potential or actual competitors, can improve firms' competitive advantage in more than one way. First, strategic alliances may facilitate entry into new markets. Second, firms create strategic alliances to share cost (and associated risks) of developing new products or processes. Third, alliances help bring together complementary knowledge, skills, abilities, and other assets that neither company could easily develop on its own. Finally, effective alliances can help firms establish technological standards for a particular market or industry—a competitive advantage that may be sustained for a long time.

As more traditional firms recognize alliances as a source of competitive advantage, there is likely to be an increase in alliances between mature and entrepreneurial firms. Thus, entrepreneurial strategies are likely not only to permeate organizational hierarchies but also to diffuse from one organization to another. This also means that scholars have the opportunity to develop new research themes to explain empirically how alliances add value and develop competitive advantage.

ATTITUDES TOWARD SMALL BUSINESSES AND INTERNATIONAL TRADE OPPORTUNITIES

Attitudes toward small business are highly favorable. A recent survey sponsored by NFIB indicated that 85% of the American public believe that small businesses have a positive influence on this country. Furthermore, 70% feel that owning a small business is one of the best ways to "get ahead" (Dennis, 1997a). These prevailing views provide psychological support for entrepreneurs as they consider whether to undertake the launching of new ventures. These attitudes also suggest that the public may be supportive of governmental initiatives to foster entrepreneurship.

Positive attitudes toward entrepreneurship create a supportive climate that makes it more likely that entrepreneurs can attract resources and receive assistance and encouragement in their ventures.

There are also increasing numbers of opportunities for entrepreneurs to do business overseas. Global trade is growing at 6% per year, more than twice as fast as the world GNP ("Inc. 500," 1997). Although historically American entrepreneurs have been less internationally minded than their counterparts in many other countries, this is beginning to change. Within the former Soviet Union, it is indeed remarkable that an activity formerly considered a criminal undertaking—entrepreneurship—is now positively encouraged and actively nurtured. These developments have implications for academic institutions doing teaching and research on entrepreneurship. According to Ballon (1998), scholars from Brigham Young University taught entrepreneurship and free enterprise at the Belorussian State Economics University in Minsk. Scholars from Case Western Reserve University helped develop a business and entrepreneurship studies program now offered by Zelenograd Business College in conjunction with Miett University in Moscow. Similar trends of educational alliances in the area of entrepreneurship are taking place between Middle Eastern and U.S. scholars as well (Bagby et al., 1998).

OPPORTUNITY BARRIERS

Within the United States, entrepreneurial strategies and new ventures are responsible for a tremendous increase in wealth and numbers of jobs. However, the benefits have not been equally distributed. Some groups, such as African Americans, Native Americans, and some Hispanics, have had lower and, on the whole, less successful rates of entrepreneurship. Whether this will change will depend on overcoming many psychological, sociological, and environmental challenges. Demographic changes (e.g., working mothers and dual-income/career workers) and institutional factors (e.g., social beliefs about women's role and work-family relations) have been associated with increased entrepreneurial activities.

Entrepreneurship can be one of the great avenues toward social advancement. Generations of immigrants have used business ownership as a way to get started. One of the challenges is how to help groups that have not had a tradition of entrepreneurship to move ahead in this way. The benefits can be broad; communities characterized with higher rates of entrepreneurship tend to experience better local economies (Flynn, 1998).

The geographic distribution of entrepreneurial activity, particularly the establishment of growth-oriented and high-tech firms, is unequally distributed. In fact, much of the entrepreneurial activity has been in the counties around metropolitan areas. The growth of telecommunications capabilities makes it possible for many entrepreneurs (and some mature organizations) to relocate. It will be interesting to see whether this will have a substantial impact on the future geographical distribution of entrepreneurial activity, social advancement, and regional wealth. As a result of these trends, we suspect that scholars will be likely to undertake new themes of research, such as nonwork relations, family-organization relations, community-organization relations, and organizational mobility, all of which are highly related to the academic study of entrepreneurship.

UNIVERSITIES AS INCUBATORS

With the emphasis in the global economy on speed, innovation, nimbleness, and particularly knowledge, many new businesses are emerging around research-based university campuses. MIT's graduates and faculty have founded 4,000 businesses, which in 1994 generated $232 billion in sales worldwide (Ballon, 1998). In Britain, Cambridge has incubated 1,200 high-tech companies (Flynn, 1998). This, in turn, reduced Cambridge's unemployment to just 2.3% and raised weekly wages (as compared to the national average) by 8%.

According to Flynn (1998), scholars capitalize on their knowledge by patenting their discoveries. This leads to start-ups and the development of entrepreneurial clusters that attract the likes of Hitachi, Xerox, Intel, and Microsoft. In Britain, as in the United States, some academics are turning themselves into successful entrepreneurs by developing innovative ideas and by facilitating the transfer of technological breakthrough from universities to industry. Some even amass fortunes by licensing their creative ideas and discoveries to established players or by starting venture-backed businesses and taking them public. In Britain, a recent count indicated at least 120 millionaire-professors (Flynn, 1998). More importantly, the benefits from incubating new start-ups encompass universities, communities, and countries. Microsoft, for example, has announced its plan to build a $80 million research lab in Cambridge (Microsoft's first non-U.S. research lab). William H. Gates III also has declared that he will commit $16 million to back community start-ups and will provide a $20-million donation for a university computer lab. In contrast, ignoring the benefits of entrepreneurship can have major consequences for an economy. A business culture hostile to entrepreneurship can push talented engineers and MBAs to vote with their feet and move. France, already struggling with more than 20% unemployment (among those under 26 years of age), experiences a "brain drain" in which up to 25% of its elite graduates are seeking employment elsewhere (Edmondson, 1998). Other French entrepreneurs and their high-tech start-ups react to the disapproving French ambience by shifting offices and operations to Silicon Valley and other knowledge centers around the world.

Entrepreneurial momentum around universities, or the lack of it, can be explained by the resource-based view of the firm. Universities are no longer places of mere passive leaning and knowledge storage but are rather turning into centers for knowledge development, acquisition, and dissemination. In other words, research universities are turning into national resources, in which they serve as "brokerages" of knowledge transfer and economic engines. This affects industry location, population distribution, and even the character of communities. These examples clearly demonstrate that entrepreneurial strategies, even within nonprofit organizations (e.g., universities), can have a significantly positive impact on their communities.

THE ROLE OF SCHOLARS OF ENTREPRENEURSHIP

We now conclude this chapter by focusing on scholars' roles in the evolution of the field of entrepreneurship. We consider teaching, career opportunities, and research and their impact on the field of entrepreneurship.

Teaching

In universities, student interest is the driving force for the development of the field (Vankataraman, 1997). If our courses are interesting and viewed as making solid contributions, then it is more likely that growth in entrepreneurship education (e.g., courses, majors, and centers) will continue. To this end, we have to continue developing good teaching materials and exciting sequences of courses. We also need to earn the support of colleagues in other fields. We should recognize that some of the leading journals have not yet published much on entrepreneurship. Furthermore, some of the strongest universities, where there are the resources to provide substantial support, have met their teaching needs primarily with adjunct faculty. For the field of entrepreneurship to be fully accepted in these settings, it must develop useful conceptual frameworks well grounded in theory. We need to develop strong empirical research that has clear implications for those who establish and build new ventures. The deepening and broadening of the intellectual foundations of our field will depend on successful research *and* course development.

Teaching, research, and support programs for entrepreneurship will more likely be supported if we can demonstrate that our academic knowledge, skills, and abilities help incubate new firms, facilitate their growth, and improve their survival rates. Our ability to guide technology transfer and to strengthen existing and emerging firms can attract resources from university administrations, corporations, and legislatures. This will require effective outreach programs and better understanding of how to educate students and prospective entrepreneurs and how to transfer and commercialize new knowledge and technology concerning entrepreneurship.

Funding and Career Opportunities

The development of university programs in entrepreneurship has been significantly affected by support from wealthy alumni (Ballon, 1998). In every university, deans are under pressure to raise money. As they talk to constituents, they discover not only that their wealthier alumni have often made their money in entrepreneurship but also that programs that promote entrepreneurial strategy and new business ventures generate the most excitement. In addition, a number of foundations have provided impressive support. The Coleman, Price, Kauffman, and NFIB Foundations have all sponsored a number of initiatives to encourage and support entrepreneurship research, education, and practice. Probably no other field of management has been so supported and influenced by foundations. Wealthy alumni and foundations have endowed many chaired professorships, helped to set up centers, and provided support in developing novel courses and outreach programs. All of this has also led to a curious development with regard to career opportunities within the field. In most academic fields, the job opportunities might be represented by a pyramid: more opportunities at the assistant professor level, followed by somewhat fewer at the associate level, and with even fewer opportunities at the full professor and chaired professor levels. In entrepreneurship, the pyramid has been upside down, with relatively few full-time opportunities for assistant professors but with many chairs unfilled. This means that although deans frequently have funding for new chairs in entrepreneurship, they find it difficult to recruit academics with the required credentials to fill those chairs.

As noted earlier, progress depends on the continuing development of the intellectual capital of the field. Many of these contributions will come from the young faculties who are entering the field with the latest training and the motivation to "make a career in entrepreneurship." There will be limited progress if we rely primarily on people who move into the field in midcareer and who lack the motivation to devote their full energies to the field. This means that there must be career opportunities for young faculty. Furthermore, they must be supported, mentored, and encouraged by deans and chairs. A flow of young, qualified faculty requires that doctoral programs be developed and supported, with the best doctoral students being actively recruited and exposed to the richness and excitement of the field. Trained in the latest research techniques, these students will provide the energy to propel the field forward.

Research

Research in entrepreneurship is attractive because it focuses on some of the central questions concerning the vitality of our economies. It is also attractive because many interesting questions have not yet been fully explored. These include "What are the processes by which new ventures are formed?" "Why are new ventures formed at certain times and places and not others?" "What factors influence the subsequent performance of new firms?" and "How can established organizations be made more innovative and entrepreneurial?" These (and other) questions have been explored with increasing sophistication, but there is still much to be done. Indeed, critics argue that the field lacks a central research paradigm, that it devotes inadequate attention to issues of validity and reliability, and that its analytical methods are crude (Amit, Glosten, & Muller, 1993; Low & MacMillan, 1988; MacMillan & Katz, 1992; Sandberg, 1992). They argue that the field doesn't even agree on definitions, including definitions of entrepreneurship (Gartner, 1988) and business failure (DeCastro, Alvarez, Blasick, & Ortiz, 1997).

How will the field develop with regard to research and writing? Aldrich and Baker (1997) noted three views of entrepreneurship research, each of which implies a different evolutionary path. The traditional path—that of a "normal science"—emphasizes empirically tested hypotheses and well-grounded theories in what might increasingly be viewed as a specialized field. A second path is a multiple-paradigm approach. It would involve research methods from a variety of disciplines, including economics, sociology, and psychology. In this view, theories might be borrowed from relevant fields, and much of the research might be published in the journals of those fields. This means that entrepreneurship journals would play a lesser role and that scholars would have to read widely to follow the work in the field. A third approach is more pragmatic and less theory driven: It considers topicality, data availability, and perceived applicability. With this approach, the primary concern would be with addressing interesting and relevant questions.

In our view, the concern for "academic respectability" and the near-universal anxiety over getting tenure may promote the first two evolutionary patterns. However, the field attracts a variety of faculties, many of whom have extensive practical experience as entrepreneurs or venture capitalists. Others are full-time academics of a practical bent, concerned with making their courses and producing relevant and immediately useful publications. This diversity of people may mean that the field will continue to be eclectic and open to a variety of theoretical and research frameworks and will continue to speak to a variety of audiences.

It seems likely that the trend toward specialization will continue as scholars concentrate on topics such as international entrepreneurship, the role of networks, or informal venture capital. We see no reason for this to change, nor do we foresee a single dominant research paradigm emerging. The richness of our field, arising out of research questions that are diverse and cross-functional, suggests that a variety of approaches to entrepreneurial research will be fruitful. The field has been noted for many large-scale projects. This is exemplified by the Entrepreneurial Research Consortium (ERC) project, which is a multiyear, multiuniversity, and multinational study. The Dun & Bradstreet/Kauffman Foundation database of 1.2 million firms is another example. Yet entrepreneurship is particularly concerned with innovative behavior and unusual achievements. Thus, small-scale studies of unusually fascinating or innovative new ventures will certainly continue to be of interest. All of this suggests that multiple patterns of development are likely to continue.

CONCLUSION

The primary objective of this chapter was to consider the evolution of entrepreneurship as an academic field of study. Therefore, we briefly reviewed its short academic history and then considered its present state and future prospects. We noted its emphasis on entrepreneurial strategies and new venture creation. It was also our objective to show how the field of entrepreneurship has over time altered the way that even established organizations develop strategy. We noted that the field's original focus was on small business management and new venture creation but that a major emphasis on developing entrepreneurial strategies in existing firms subsequently emerged. This chapter also suggested that the development of the field has implications for entrepreneurs, public policy and strategy makers, managers, and even the general public. We concluded the chapter with three sections focusing on scholars' roles in the evolution of the field of entrepreneurship and suggested that eclectic paradigms and research are likely to continue. Clearly, the field, its methods, and the topics of research are still under construction. There is ambiguity and change, which may seem to reflect a lack of clear organization. However, there is also energy and dynamism. The field of entrepreneurship is young, and there is still much to be done (Cooper, Hornaday, & Vesper, 1997).

REFERENCES

Acs, Z. J. (1996). Innovation: Largely the work of small firms. *Small Business Advocate, 15*(8), 11.

Aldrich, H. E., & Baker, T. (1997). Blinded by the cites? Has there been progress in entrepreneurship research? In D. L. Sexton & R. W. Smilor (Eds.), *Entrepreneurship 2000*. Chicago: Upstart.

Amit, R., Glosten, L., & Muller, E. (1993). Challenges to theory development in entrepreneurship research. *Journal of Management Studies, 30*, 815-834.

Bagby, R., Brockhaus, J., Francis, D., Giamartino, G., Gillman, J., Learned, K., Matthews, C., Meyer, G. D., Richards, J., Unni, V. K., & Wojtasz, E. (1998, January). *Small and family business in Saudi Arabia and Bahrain: Challenges and opportunities*. Paper presented at the 12th

Annual National Conference of the U.S. Association of Small Business and Entrepreneurship, Clearwater, FL.

Ballon, M. (1998). Campus Inc. *Inc Magazine, 3,* 36-52.

Baron, R. A., & Markman, G. D. (In press). Beyond social capital: The role of social competence in entrepreneurs' success. *Academy of Management Executive.*

Byrne, J. A. (1994, May 9). The pain of downsizing. *Business Week,* pp. 60-68.

Cascio, W. F. (1993, February). Downsizing: What do we know? What have we learned? *Academy of Management Executive, 7,* 95-104.

Champy, J. (1995). *Reengineering management.* New York: Harper-Collins.

Cooper, A. C. (1964, May-June). R&D is more efficient in small companies. *Harvard Business Review, 42,* 75-83.

Cooper, A. C., Hornaday, J. A., & Vesper, K. H. (1997). The field of entrepreneurship over time. In P. D. Reynolds, W. D. Bygrave, N. M. Carter, P. Davidsson, W. Gartner, C. M. Mason, & P. P. McDougall (Eds.), *Frontiers of entrepreneurship research.* Wellesley, MA: Babson College, Center for Entrepreneurial Studies.

Corporate almanac. (1996). Cambridge, MA: Cognetics.

D'Aveni, R. A. (1994). *Hyper-competition: Managing the dynamics of strategic maneuvering.* New York: Free Press.

Dean, T. J., Meyer, G. D., & DeCastro, J. (1993). Determinants of new-firm formations in manufacturing industries: Industry dynamics, entry barriers, and organizational inertia. *Entrepreneurship Theory and Practice, 17*(2), 49-60.

DeCastro, J., Alvarez, S., Blasick, J., & Ortiz, M. (1997). An examination of the nature of business closings: Are they really failures? In P. D. Reynolds, W. D. Bygrave, N. M. Carter, P. Davidsson, W. Gartner, C. M. Mason, & P. P. McDougall (Eds.), *Frontiers of entrepreneurship research.* Wellesley, MA: Babson College, Center for Entrepreneurial Studies.

Dennis, W. J., Jr. (1997a). More than you think: An inclusive estimate of business entries. *Journal of Business Venturing, 12,*(3), 175-196.

Dennis, W. J., Jr. (1997b). *The public reviews small business.* Washington, DC: National Federation of Independent Business, Education Foundation.

Edmondson, G. (1998, March 9). Go west, young Frenchman, *Business Week,* p. 52.

Flynn, J. (1998, March 9). Millionaire dons. *Business Week,* pp. 98-101.

Gartner, W. B. (1988). "Who is an entrepreneur?" is the wrong question. *Entrepreneurship Theory and Practice, 13*(4), 47-68.

Hitt, M. A., & Bartkus, B. R. (1997). International entrepreneurship. In J. A. Katz & R. H. Brockhaus, Sr. (Eds.), *Advances in entrepreneurship, firm emergence, and growth.* Greenwich, CT: JAI.

Hitt, M. A., & Ireland, R. D. (1987). Peters and Waterman revisited: The unended quest for excellence. *Academy of Management Executive, 1*(2), 91-98.

Inc. 500: The 1997 ranking of the fastest-growing private companies in America. (1997, October). *Inc.,* pp. 145-181.

Ireland, R. D., & Hitt, M. A. (1997). Performance strategies for high-growth entrepreneurial firms. In P. D. Reynolds, W. D. Bygrave, N. M. Carter, P. Davidsson, W. Gartner, C. M. Mason, & P. P. McDougall (Eds.), *Frontiers of entrepreneurship research.* Wellesley, MA: Babson College, Center for Entrepreneurial Studies.

Katz, J. A. (1997, August). *Report to the Academy Professional Division Review Committee: A five-year review of the Entrepreneurship Division of the Academy of Management.* Paper presented at the annual meeting of the Academy of Management, Boston.

Low, M. B., & MacMillan, I. C. (1988). Entrepreneurship: Past research and future challenges. *Journal of Management, 14,* 139 161.

MacMillan, I. C., & Katz, J. A. (1992). Idiosyncratic milieus of entrepreneurial research: The need for comprehensive theories. *Journal of Business Venturing, 7,* 1-8.

Maney, K. (1994, March 24). High price of layoffs. *USA Today,* p. 6B.

Miles, R. E., & Snow, C. C. (1986). Organizations: New concepts for new forms. *California Management Review, 28*(3), 62-73.

Peters, T. J., & Waterman, R. H., Jr. (1984). *In search of excellence.* New York: Warner.

Rousseau, D. M. (1997). Organizational behavior in the new organizational era. *Annual Review of Psychology, 48,* 515-546.

Sandberg, W. R. (1992, Spring). Strategic management's potential contributions to a theory of entrepreneurship. *Entrepreneurship Theory and Practice, 16,* 73-90.

Schmit, J. (1994, January 20). AMR quarterly loss totals $253 million. *USA Today,*, p. 2B.

Sookdeo, R. (1992, July 27). Why to buy big in bad times. *Fortune,* p. 96.

Venkataraman, S. (1997). The distinctive domain of entrepreneurship research. *Advances in Entrepreneurship, Firm Emergence and Growth, 3,* 119-138.

Venkataraman, S. (In press). *The distinctive domain of entrepreneurship research: An editor's perspective.* Working Paper, Rensselaer Polytechnic Institute.

Vesper, K. H. (1993). *Entrepreneurship education 1993,* Los Angeles: Entrepreneurial Studies Center, University of California, Los Angeles.

Weick, K. E. (1996). Enactment and the boundaryless career: Organizing as we work. In M. B. Arthur & D. M. Rousseau (Eds.), *The boundaryless career: A new employment principle for a new organizational era* (pp. 40-57). New York: Oxford University Press.

Welsch, H. P., & Klandt, H. (1997). *International entrepreneurship and small business bibliography* (2nd ed.). Washington, DC: National Federation of Independent Business.

Who's creating jobs? (1996). Cambridge, MA: Cognetics.

Zahra, S. A. (1996). Environment, corporate entrepreneurship, and financial performance: A taxonomic approach. *Journal of Business Venturing, 8,* 319-340.

Index

About the Editors

G. Dale Meyer is the Ted G. Anderson Professor of Entrepreneurial Development and Executive Director of the Robert H. and Beverly A. Deming Center for Entrepreneurship at the Graduate School of Business, University of Colorado at Boulder. He is Professor of Strategic Management/ Entrepreneurship and holds the lifetime designation of President's Teaching Scholar. In 1998, he won the Hazel Barnes Prize, the university's highest career achievement award, for the combination of teaching and research. He has published more than 70 refereed academic articles in major and specialized journals, including the *Academy of Management Journal, Administrative Science Quarterly, Journal of Business Venturing, Entrepreneurship Theory and Practice, Journal of Business Ethics,* and Babson's *Frontiers of Entrepreneurship Research.* He serves on several journal editorial boards and is author of the book *Participative Decision Making.* In 1997, he received the Career Mentor Award from the Entrepreneurship Division of the Academy of Management. He is past President of the U.S. Association for Small Business and Entrepreneurship (USASBE), past Chair of the Entrepreneurship Division of the Academy of Management, and President-Elect of the International Council for Small Business (ICSB).

Kurt A. Heppard is Assistant Professor of Management at the U.S. Air Force Academy in Colorado. His research interests include interorganizational strategies, entrepreneurship, and organizational communication. His publications include "Deviance From Normality or the Normalization of Deviance" with P. K. Tompkins and C. Melville (in *Organization*) and "High Expectations, Supportiveness, and the Management Hall of Fame" (in *Journal of Management Inquiry*). He has made a number of conference presentations, including ones at the Strategic Management Society and the Academy of Management Annual Meetings for the past several years. His current research focuses on interorganizational adaptation, entrepreneurial competencies, and concertive control in organizations. He received a BS from the U.S. Air Force Academy, an MBA from the Anderson Graduate School of Management at the University of California at Los Angeles, and a PhD in business policy and strategy from the University of Colorado at Boulder in 1998.

About the Contributors

Sharon Alvarez is Visiting Assistant Professor of Entrepreneurship and Strategy at the Max M. Fisher College of Business at Ohio State University, where she is doing a 2-year postdoctorate with Professor Jay Barney. She holds a master's of international management (international MBA) from the University of Denver and a PhD from the University of Colorado in strategy and entrepreneurship. Her current research includes alliances between entrepreneurial firms and larger established firms, business closures and failures, complexity theory in the use of innovation, entrepreneurial decision making, and women entrepreneurs.

Raphael H. Amit is the Robert B. Goergen Professor of Entrepreneurship and Professor of Management at the Wharton School, where he is also the Academic Director of the Goergen Entrepreneurial Management Program. Previously, he was the Peter Wall Distinguished Professor at the Faculty of Commerce and Business Administration, University of British Columbia (UBC), where he was the founding director of the W. Maurice Young Entrepreneurship and Venture Capital Research Center. Between 1983 and 1990, he was on the faculty of the J. L. Kellogg Graduate School of Management at Northwestern University, where he was the recipient of the J. L. Kellogg Research Professorship and the Richard M. Paget Research Chair in Business Policy. He holds an MA degree in economics and received his PhD in management from Northwestern University. He serves on the editorial boards of the *Strategic Management Journal, Organization Science,* and the *Journal of Business Venturing.* His research and teaching interests center on entrepreneurship in independent and corporate settings and on strategic management. His academic research is published in the *Academy of Management Journal, California Management Review, Journal of Economic Behavior and Organization, Journal of Business Venturing, Journal of Management, Management Science, Operations Research, Strategic Management Journal,* and others.

Jay Barney is Professor of Management and holds the Bank One Chair for Excellence in Corporate Strategy at the Max M. Fisher College of Business at Ohio State University. He received his master's and doctorate from Yale University. He has also served on the faculty at the Anderson Graduate School of Management at the University of California at Los Angeles and at Texas A&M University. In his research, he focuses on the relationship between idiosyncratic firm skills and capabilities and sustained competitive advantage.

Keith Brigham is a doctoral candidate in business policy and strategy at the University of Colorado at Boulder, where he earned his MBA. He has taught several courses on entrepreneurship and small business strategy. He has presented at the Academy of Management annual meetings and at Strategic Management Society meetings. His current research projects focus on habitual entrepreneurs, growth stage implications, and innovation. He has experience as a manager and has founded and successfully grown several new ventures.

Shona L. Brown is a Senior Engagement Manager in the Toronto office of McKinsey & Company. Her client work has focused on industries that are technology based and/or consumer focused. Recent study experiences include designing a growth program for a logistics company, assisting a major bank with the design and implementation of a substantial change management program, developing business strategies for e-commerce, and helping the internal board of a global health care company identify ways to develop world-class operations. Her expertise is centered broadly on the management of innovation, strategy, and marketing in highly uncertain, rapidly changing markets. She is the author of numerous academic articles appearing in leading management journals (including *Harvard Business Review*). In addition, she is the author of *Competing on the Edge: Strategy as Structured Chaos,* which introduces a new strategic paradigm for competing in volatile markets. She completed a PhD and did postdoctoral work at Stanford University and also holds an MA in economics and philosophy from Oxford University.

Arnold C. Cooper is the Louis A. Weil, Jr. Professor of Management at the Krannert Graduate School of Management, Purdue University. He was the 1997 recipient of the International Award in Small Business Research and Entrepreneurship. In 1999, he received the Richard D. Irwin Outstanding Educator Award from the Division of Business Policy and Strategy of the Academy of Management. His research has been published in a number of journals, including *Journal of Business Venturing, Strategic Management Journal,* and *Administrative Science Quarterly.* He has been a member of the faculty or a visiting scholar at the Harvard Business School, Stanford University, the Wharton School, the IMD Management Development Institute, and the Manchester Business School. He has received numerous teaching and research awards during his 39-year career.

Kathleen M. Eisenhardt is Professor of Strategy and Organization at Stanford University. Her interests center on strategy and organization in high velocity industries. She has worked extensively with many firms, especially in computing, telecommunications, and networking, software, and semi-conductor industries. Her theoretical interests are in complexity and evolutionary theories. She is coauthor of *Competing on the Edge: Strategy at the Edge of Structured Chaos* (1998). She has published articles in various academic journals, including *Organization Science, Administrative Science Quarterly, Strategic Management Journal,* and *Academy of Management Review.*

Michael A. Hitt is Distinguished Professor of Management and holds the Paul M. and Rosalie Robertson Chair of Business Administration at Texas A&M University. He is the author or coauthor of over 150 publications, including books, book chapters, and articles in such journals as the *Academy of Management Journal, Strategic Management Journal,* and *Academy of Management Review.* Among his 14 books are such recent ones as *Strategic Management: Competitiveness and Globalization, Managing Strategically in an Interconnected World, New Managerial Mindsets: Organizational Transformation and Strategy Implementation,* and *Dynamic Strategic Resources: Development, Diffusion and Integration.*

He has also written a forthcoming book on mergers and acquisitions. He is the former editor of the *Academy of Management Journal* and past President of the Academy of Management. Currently, he serves on the Board of the Strategic Management Society. He received the award for outstanding academic contributions to competitiveness from the American Society for Competitiveness in 1996 and received an honorary doctorate from the Universidad Carlos III de Madrid in 1999.

Gideon D. Markman is Assistant Professor of Entrepreneurship at the Lally School of Management and Technology at Rensselaer Polytechnic Institute (the first degree-granting technological university in the English-speaking world). He received his PhD in entrepreneurship from the University of Colorado at Boulder. His research interests include innovation management and technological entrepreneurship. Specifically, his empirical and conceptual work focuses on entrepreneurs' adversity quotient, cognitive mechanisms, and social skills. His work has been published in the *Academy of Management Journal* and the *Academy of Management Executive*, and his research on entrepreneurs' social skills was recently featured in *Business Week*. He has presented his empirical and theoretical work at numerous conferences, including the Academy of Management, British Academy of Management, and Babson College-Kauffman Foundation Entrepreneurship Research Conference.

Grant Miles is Assistant Professor in the Department of Management at the University of North Texas, where he teaches courses in the areas of organization theory and strategic management. His research interests include the study of industry variety, alliances and networks, and organizational form. His publications include articles in the *Strategic Management Journal, Journal of Business Ethics,* and *Academy of Management Executive.* He earned his PhD at Pennsylvania State University.

Raymond E. Miles is Trefethen Professor Emeritus and former Dean at the Water A. Haas School of Business at the University of California, Berkeley. His research and writing over the past 40 years have covered a wide variety of topics, ranging from leadership to strategy-structure fit to new organizational forms. He has served as a consultant to educational, business, and governmental organizations in the United States, Asia, and Europe. He is the coauthor of *Organizational Strategy, Structure, and*

Process and *Fit, Failure, and the Hall of Fame,* as well as three other books, and is a frequent contributor to leading professional journals.

Heidi M. Neck is currently pursuing a PhD in strategic management and entrepreneurship from the University of Colorado at Boulder. She holds an MBA in organization management and entrepreneurship from the University of Colorado at Boulder. Her research emphasizes the entrepreneurial firm, focusing on new venture creation and growth, incubator organizations, entrepreneurial teams, and initial public offerings. She has presented at numerous conferences, including the Academy of Management annual meetings, the U.S. Association for Small Business and Entrepreneurship (USASBE), and the Babson-Kauffman Entrepreneurship Research Conference. She has published in *Frontiers of Entrepreneurship Research,* the *Journal of Developmental Entrepreneurship,* and the *Journal of Leadership Studies.* She has consulted for several emerging growth companies in Colorado and has worked 4 years for the Dow Chemical Company.

Gayle Niss is a Managing Partner of Colorado Storage Solutions, LLC. She has been a research and editorial assistant on *Web Farming* and an entrepreneur for over 20 years. She also teaches business strategy in industry. Her research interests are in managing growth within entrepreneurial companies.

Timothy S. Reed is a major in the U.S. Air Force and is a doctoral candidate pursuing a PhD in business policy and strategy under an Air Force scholarship at the University of Colorado at Boulder. He earned a master's degree in administration from Central Michigan University. His research emphasizes the effects of legitimacy on entrepreneurial firm initial public offerings and international cooperative agreements. He has presented his research at the Strategic Management Society, the Academy of International Business, the International Association of Management, and the Academy of Management annual meetings.

Charles C. Snow is Professor of Business Administration and Mellon Bank Faculty Fellow at the University of Pennsylvania. His research has focused on competitive strategy and its implications for organization design and human resource management. He has published articles on strategy and organization in the *Academy of Management Journal, Academy of Management Review, Administrative Science Quarterly, California Management Review, Journal of Management Studies, Organizational Science,* and *Strategic Management Journal.* He has coauthored a number of influential books, including *Organizational Strategy, Structure, and Process* and *Fit, Failure, and the Hall of Fame.*

Printed in the United States
By Bookmasters